GW00372230

The Pocket Guide to Hunting

Copyright © Losange, 1999

Editor: Hervé Chaumeton
Photography: Stéphanie Henry, Véronique Janvier, Chantal Mialon
Project Coordination: Muriel Bresson

Original title: *Mini-guide de la Chasse*

Copyright © 2000 for this English revised edition:
Könemann Verlagsgesellschaft mbH
Bonner Strasse 126, D – 50968 Cologne

Translation from French: Translate-A-Book, Oxford, UK
Project Coordination: Alex Morkramer
Production Manager: Ursula Schümer

Printing and Binding: Star Standard Industries Ltd.
Printed in Singapore

ISBN 3-8290-4351-1
10 9 8 7 6 5 4 3 2 1

The Pocket Guide to Hunting

Georges Cortay
Pascal Durantel
Eric Joly
François Pasquet
Claude Rossignol

KÖNEMANN

CONTENTS

Introduction

Mature stag at the height of his powers. Today, big game is making a great comeback throughout Europe.

The first men were hunters from the beginning. In those days, the art of hunting amounted simply to a matter of predation: people had to kill – and sometimes risk their own lives – to feed the clan. The weapons of the time consisted of clubs, stone axes, or spears hardened by fire; pathetic weapons for taking on cave bears, European bison, and saber-toothed tigers.

To subsist, hunting peoples were compelled to live nomadic lives when prey became rare or difficult to catch. They began to search for new territories, following moving herds of reindeer, for example. Eventually, hunting was no longer necessary for the survival of these itinerant clans. They settled down, learning how to farm and raise animals. Hunting had not yet become a leisure activity. In a sense, it was a kind of self-affirmation, with the hunter proving his strength and courage in front of the others. When not at war, these clans tracked bear, wolf, and bison. These were some of the many coveted trophies with which the hunters could enhance their reputations. A great hunter was inevitably also a redoubtable warrior. Thus, he became a man worthy of the trust of others who could one day hold the title of clan chieftain. The real value of the day was

Today, hunting has attracted more and more followers, as much devoted to chamois as to stag, roebuck, sheep, or wild boar.

Introduction

This fine retriever poses before the local game, a hare with its pale, winter coloring.

people with a handle to their names were allowed to be landowners and thus hunters. Weapons were improved, and animals were no longer faced with bare hands or a spear but with a bow or crossbow. Hunting became sophisticated, viewed as suitable for courtly gatherings. This period saw the birth of the hunt as well as falconry, practiced with an equal passion by both lords and ladies.

This obscure time in the history of the Old Continent, when the nobility appropriated for itself the exclusive right to hunt, was not without positive consequence for the future of wildlife in general.

measured in terms of wild animals killed, not in those of philosophical discussions or coin of the realm.

During the Middle Ages, hunting experienced a true upheaval. At first a survival activity, then a sometimes-cruel game by which men established themselves in the heart of a community, hunting finally became a leisure activity. It was also an expensive one, reserved for those few privileged people who belonged to the nobility. Only those

For this nobility to indulge its veritable passion for hunting, there had to be game. It had to be protected and its environment preserved.

If we benefit today from these superb forest, planted all across Europe, it is partly due to the policies pursued by the medieval lords who forbade excessive deforestation so that they could have a place to hunt. Today, hunting is far more than a simple leisure activity. It requires a sound sense of ecology in managing both the animal populations and the land. The modern hunter is permanently concerned about protecting both the game and the ecosystem.

Even though we talk about making constant efforts to defend wildlife, we must also point out that hunting fulfills a specific desire. This is the healthy, natural, human desire to revive an instinct weakened by civilizations that have become artificial.

The laws governing nature depend upon the constant interaction of the forces of life and death. The important thing for the hunter to know is that he does not play out of tune in this vital concert, but that he plays, with fervor, from a score that rings true.

In this second millennium, now that man has walked on the Moon and even invented the atomic bomb, it gladdens the heart to know that there are still communities – like the Inuit or Native Americans of North America, the Aborigines of Australia, the Bushmen of the Kalahari,

and the Pygmies in the forests of the Congo – whose survival depends entirely on hunting. These peoples have successfully preserved the precious heritage represented by wildlife since the dawn of time.

Back from a partridge shoot in Beauce, France's great cereal-growing plain. Despite the practice of agriculture, there is still an abundance of game.

GUNS,
AMMUNITION,
AND ACCESSORIES

Smoothbore Guns

If we consider the numerous combinations of barrel configurations, breechloading systems, locks, and firing mechanisms, the range is immense. Because there has been such prolific innovation in these areas, we will deal only with the types most frequently encountered.

OVER-AND-UNDER DOUBLE-BARRELED GUNS

The configuration of over-and-under double-barreled guns enjoyed a certain success at the beginning of the 18th century, then faded almost to extinction during the reign of Napoleon I at the beginning of the 19th century. Over-and-unders made a permanent comeback before the prosperous years of the 1930s, probably stimulated by the appearance of the remarkable B25 of John Browning (the pioneer of modern guns was never able to enjoy seeing his designs brought to fruition: he died in Herstal, Belgium, in the fall of 1926). The development of pigeon shooting also weighed much in favor of this kind of gun. More prosaically, we must not forget the considerable financial effects of a new fashion.

Today, all of the big manufacturers make over-and-unders. Their intrinsic designs seem particularly suited to automated industrial production.

Petrik over-and-under shotgun with sidelock style action and false lockplates.

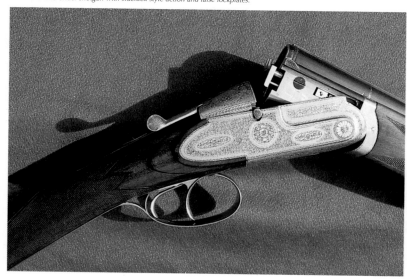

Detailed view of the ejectors and the lower locking groove (Browning barrels).

The followers of this system prefer single sight plane. They also prefer handling characteristics that are more biased toward the muzzles. There are two drawbacks that, while not crippling, are certainly real:

– The vertical setup of the barrels puts a greater strain on the locking system.

– This setup makes the gun more sensitive when held at a slant.

In terms of aesthetics, there is clearly nothing to argue about, though the allure of certain weapons at the top of the range (such as those made by Boss or Abbiatico & Salvinelli) can be quite strong.

SIDE-BY-SIDE DOUBLE-BARRELED GUNS

Side-by-side double-barreled guns embody the great traditions of gunmaking, with a silhouette that is considered to be of the finest pedigree. They offer the further advantage of sitting more comfortably on the forearm.

They are usually furnished with two types of mechanism, which have numerous derivatives: the Blitz action, whose principal parts are operated through the trigger guard, and the seminal Anson & Deeley action. In 1875, these two English gunmakers patented the best of the modern "hammerless" systems (without external hammers) that we recognize today. This type of action is extremely simple and therefore reliable. In addition, it can be cocked without great effort by the fall of the barrels

Smoothbore Guns

SIDELOCK GUNS

The lockplates are the two plates that are fixed to either side of the stock to which the firing mechanism is attached.

Having a good gun with sidelocks does not imply a significant gain in ballistic performance. It is simply about possessing a deluxe, personalized weapon whose finish brings a unique feeling that only the well-informed and well-off *aficionado* is aware of. More than ever, mediocrity and bad taste are unbearable in such matters. The English engraving styles, "Old English" or "Royal," found on the legendary Purdey or Holland & Holland guns provide the ideal illustration of the discreet charm of true nobility. The scrolls of very fine acanthus-leaf

cocking indicator

Merkel lockplate gun with loading indicator.

foliage, executed with a burin in the workshop, contrasting with leafy shades and hollowed backgrounds, are truly regal; they evoke an artistic mastery bordering on the sublime. The French school has no reason to envy English gunmaking in these finest of crafted products, and neither do the Belgian or the Italian schools.

Let us conclude with two essential points about the mechanical side:
– The mechanism of a sidelock gun has a smoothness and regularity that is quite without equal. In addition, it is possible to modify the characteristics.
– The design makes for a very strong action and also makes the "breaking" of the barrels more fluid and effortless (a Purdey sidelock is cocked as the breech closes). The barrel assembly (the key element) is more rigid and offers greater longevity. This, added to the

Older-model Purdey fitted with exterior hammers and damascus twist barrels.

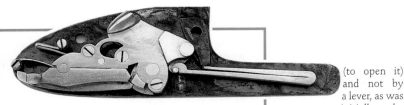

Gold plating on the hammers and triggers is no doubt aesthetic, but above all it helps to prevent oxidation.

extremely high quality of the fittings, means an expectation to fire from 100,000 to 150,000 cartridges without needing a rebore – that is, of course, with a gun from one of the most prestigious manufacturers.

(to open it) and not by a lever, as was initially the case. The cock-load-fire system consists of four moving parts, plus springs, sears and triggers. It is easy to see why every gunmaker wanted to build the Anson & Deeley action, which is fitted to about 90 percent of all side-by-side guns.

Holland & Holland hand detachable sidelock with screw.

SINGLE-BARRELED GUNS
The semi-automatic weapons

The semi-automatic system works by exploiting energy from the explosion of the cartridge, a delay in the opening of the breech (after the gas pressure has fallen to the safe level).

The successive sequences are extraction, ejection, cocking, and chambering of a new cartridge. The motive power needed to make

The carving of the stock, destined to receive the firing mechanism, is a marvel of precision handicraft.

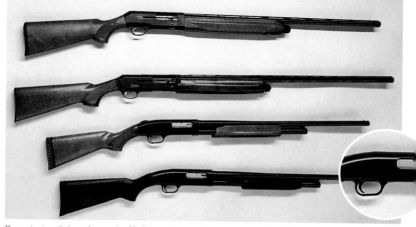

The semi-automatic is much appreciated by hunters of wildfowl (marshland and seashore). The pump-action system is even more reliable.

these pieces work can come from using gases at one point in the barrel, from the long or short recoil of the barrel, or even from an inertial system. The last, introduced by Benelli, has the immense advantage of both using a minimum of components and of still functioning properly, regardless of the load.

Apart from the very strange and luxurious breechloading Cosmi, these "ultraindustrial" guns offer nothing in the way of elegance or balance. Loading and unloading is complicated and noisy, and certain models are prone to jamming. In addition, their total lengths affects ease of handling. From the safety standpoint, these guns do not break as all of the side-by-sides and over-and-unders do. It is

therefore not easy for others on a shoot to see whether the chamber or the magazine is empty. In terms of advantages, the semiautomatics are very easy to aim, have good ballistic performance (excellent for shooting with slugs), and can fire three shots in succession.

Finally, these inexpensive guns have a number of different, interchangeable barrels for use in woodland and in open country, as well as for waterfowl, therefore offering great versatility for hunters who do not wish to own several guns.

Manual-repeating guns
The pump-action system
For guns that use the pumpaction system, the energy needed for the different sequences (mentioned

above with the semiautomatic) is provided by the shooter via the moveable fore-end.

Used by responsible hunters, these are guns like no others, highly effective with advantages of their own. In Europe, they are used mainly self-defense. In France, there is ill-considered legislation poised to bring about the total eradication of these guns.

The Mauser-type bolt system
In Europe, a gun that uses the Mauser-type bolt system is not often encountered, as it is chiefly used on the seashores of the United States. Its success seems essentially linked to an extremely attractive price, which does not deter people from using it despite the inescapable damage caused by a salty

atmosphere eating away at the metal.

THE GAUGES OF SMOOTHBORE GUNS

Gauge is expressed in an antiquated terminology inherited from the British artillery of the 17th century. It registers the number of spherical bullets (with the diameter of the barrel) contained in one old pound (0.4895 kg) of pure lead (density = 11.35). Thus, for a 12 gauge, you can make 12 bullets at 18.5 mm (0,729") in diameter with one pound of lead. During the 18th century,

Cartridges for 12, 16, 20, and 24 gauge.

people in Europe hunted with small-gauge guns, such as 24 or 28 gauge. At the beginning of the 19th century, the brilliant English gunmaker Joseph Manton

STANDARD GAUGES

Bore	4	8	10	12	14	16	20	24	28	32	36 or 12 mm or 410
Diameter of gauge: mm in. (")	23.75 0.935"	21.2 0.835"	19.5 0.768"	18.5 0.728"	17.6 0.693"	17.0 0.669"	15.7 0.618"	14.7 0.579"	14.0 0.552"	12.75 0.502"	10.41 0.410"

Depending on country and manufacturer, these diameters can vary up to 0.6 mm.

STANDARD CHOKE FOR A 12 GAUGE

Diameter of gauge	Constriction: 1/23	Full Choke	3/4 Choke	1/2 Choke	1/4 Choke	Improved cylinder
18.5 mm 0.729"	0.80 mm 0.031"	17.70 mm 0.696"	17.90 mm 0.704"	18.10mm 0.712"	18.30 mm 0.720"	18.40 mm 0.724"
		maximum range	←	effect of the choke	→	maximum spread

Smoothbore Guns

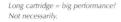

Long cartridge = big performance? Not necessarily.

(who once had James Purdey as a pupil) brought about the permanent supremacy of the 12 gauge, the effectiveness of which was confirmed by the practice of pigeon shooting after Manton's death.

Its superiority over the 16 gauge, and thus over the 20 gauge, is undeniable. This assertion is not unwarranted: the amount of shot per cartridge and experience on the ground have long proved it. Despite everything, this does not, *a priori*, make masochists of the owners of 20 gauges: their guns are lighter and more elegant than a "Big 12," they go up to the shoulder more rapidly, and above all, the extra skill they demand is rewarded by a tenfold satisfaction when a bird finally falls.

THE SHOT PATTERN

Around 1870, a principle known in former times was applied to improve shot patterns. This method consisted of reducing shot spread by introducing a constriction, the choke, at the end of the barrel. We know that shot spreads in the form of an oval cloud of variable length and height. Its length can be from 1 m (at 20 m) up to about 3 m (at 40 m). The more choke applied, the more the oval profile of the swarm of shot is flattened, and the shot

pattern is held together. The greater the diameter of the shot, the less the impact of

A load of 32–34 g seems ideal for a 12–70 gauge.

the choke, particularly from 3 mm upward (No. 5).

If the full choke suits wildfowling, the improved cylinder will also perform with woodcock in undergrowth.

But beware: the obsession with the hypothetical extreme-range shot gives a lot of woodland fans an attack of the "full-choke

Size of shot	Diameter		Average weight of shot (in g)	Number of grains (32 g load, 1 1/8 03)	Number of grains (36 g load, 1 1/4 03)
	in mm	in in.			
	1.25	0.05	0.012	2900	3270
	1.75	0.07	0.030	1050	1160
	2.00	0.08	0.047	680	765
	2.25	0.09	0.068	480	535
	2.41	0.095	0.081	390	440
	2.50	0.098	0.093	350	390
	2.75	0.108	0.123	260	295
	3.00	0.118	0.159	200	227
	3.25	0.128	0.200	160	177
	3.50	0.137	0.254	125	141
	3.75	0.148	0.313	100	117
	4.00	0.158	0.371	85	95
	4.25	0.167	0.454	70	81
	4.50	0.177	0.535	59	65
	4.75	0.187	0.636	51	57
	5.00	0.197	0.738	43	48

The "good old Brenneke slug," made since 1898.

shots. The 1/4–3/4 pairing, for example, is suitable for 90 percent of hunting situations in open terrain.

A 20-gauge Brenneke slug, found in a wild boar shot at around 15 meters.

We add several general remarks to bring this chapter to a close:

Blondeau slug: excellent precision and stopping power but incompatible with over-choked barrels.

mania." This is a gross mistake, the principal result of which is to miss the easy

Smoothbore Guns

COMPARATIVE SHOT SIZES

Diameter in mm	France	Britain	Germany	Belgium	United States
			Table of numbers		
5.00	4/0	AA	4/0	5/0	0
4.75	3/0		3/0	4/0	BBB
4.50	2/0	A	2/0	3/0	BB
4.25	0	BBB	0	2/0	–
4.00	1	BB	1	0	1
3.75	2	B	2	1	2
3.65	–	1	–	–	–
3.50	3	2	3	2	3
3.25	4	3	4	3	4
3.00	5	4	5	4	5
2.85		4 1/2			
2.80		5			6
2.75	6	5 1/2	6	5	
2.50	7	6 1/2	7	6	7
2.40	7 1/2	7		7	7 1/2
2.25	8	8	8	8	8
2.10	8 1/2				
2.00	9	9	9	9	9
1.75	10	10	10	10	10
1.70		11			
1.50	11	12	11	11	11

– Ballistics is not an exact science: certain guns with less choke perform quite remarkably at long range without anyone knowing why; others are better suited to this or that shot number, also for no apparent reason.

– Shot spread can be affected by a bad mix of size and roundness of shot, by the nature of the wadding or the crimping, and by too-high or irregular muzzle velocities, with all that this implies in terms of pressure, gun fatigue, and poor recoil. The standard muzzle velocities

Consistency is what good shooters strive for. To achieve it, they must always stick to the same make of cartridge and shot size.

are generally supersonic, be-tween 370 (1200 ft/sec) and 400 m/s (1300 ft/sec). The "souped up" performances (such as 480 m/s or 1570 ft/sec) claimedby some gun-makers should not delude anyone, how-ever, because the aerodynamic effect on the shot spread is absolutely disastrous.

– The 12/76 mm (or 12/3") Magnum car-tridges are rather dis-appointing in respect to their price and the amount of recoil they cause. In effect, you need an increase in shot weight of 28 percent (46 g as opposed to 36 g) to obtain an increase in range of 7 percent (48 m as opposed to 45 m).

– Granted, the extra-long head on certain cartridges is aesthet-ically flattering, but it will never match up to its pretensions. Actually, it is only the price that in-creases.

– Interchangeable chokes often produce unconvincing returns and must be stripped off, cleaned, and

oiled each time they are used. There are no excep-tions to this – otherwise, a blockage may result in the near future.

Shooting game is an unending lesson in humility.

Guns with Rifled Barrels

Although it was used by some in the 17th century, the rifled barrel developed significantly only during the first half of the 19th century, thanks to improvements in the techniques of cutting grooves.

You will recall that the principle of the rifled tube is to impart rotation to the projectile by helical guidance, which produces the right gyroscopic stability for considerably improving its precision and range. The muzzle velocities obtained are between 700 (2290 ft/sec) and 1200 m/s (3925 ft/sec) (for shoulder arms), and the

The bullet acquires its characteristic spin with these spiraling grooves.

Double-barreled Caliber 9.3 x 74R Express rifle.

Today, all of the big gunmakers produce repeater rifles.

of ammunition, covering the entire span of present-day hunting from crow to elephant.

Properly made, their breech-blocks never wear out and can tolerate far more than might be imagined with

projectile's rotary speed can vary between 180,000 and 230,000 rev/min. Finally, the resulting pressures are sometimes close to 4000 bars and are thus much higher than the 700 bars of the smoothbore gun. As a group, rifle firearms offer an extremely wide range of choice, as much for the guns themselves as for the plethora of ammunition available today. We will look at four major families of rifles, followed by a section where the two categories are mixed.

REPEATER RIFLES

The shooter operates a bolt-action repeater rifle manually, moving and rotating the breechblock. These are definitely the most commonly used and least expensive rifles (in the standard range). They have descended directly or indirectly from the highly celebrated Mauser mechanism of 1898. All arms manufacturers make this type of weapon, suitable for loading with a huge variety

The track of the grooves is calculated according to the speed and weight of the projectiles.

today's high-pressure cartridges. Furthermore, they do not tend to jam which adds security when you have to reload quickly to face the charge of a wounded animal.

While on this subject, we will mention the new in-line weapon (with no rotation of the lever) recently created in

Certain bolt action rifles offer the advantage of having interchangeable barrels.

Guns with Rifled Barrels

Germany by both Blaser and Mauser. Through its simplified action, this gun provides a little more time for the shooter.

These two manufacturers, in addition to the Sauer company, also produce systems with interchangeable barrels in the two main classes of caliber: medium (e.g., .243 Win. and .270 Win.) and Magnum (e.g., .7 Rem. and .375 H&H). This has the essential advantage of extending the range of use while maintaining the same shoulder position.

To close the subject of bolt-action rifles, let us mention the all-weather type, which attracts an increasing number of followers, chiefly in the United States, where aesthetic matters follow a different course than do European tastes. In this context, the choice of materials depends upon three criteria: a maximum resistance to shock, immunity to aggressive outside agents (such as rain and mud), and colors which blend in with the natural scenery. The stocks are therefore made of

carbon fiber, glass fiber, or Kevlar®, and the combination of breech and barrel can be treated with phosphates or, even better yet, coated with Teflon®, whose anti-friction properties are increasingly desirable in hostile conditions.

LEVER ACTION RIFLES

Rifles with trigger-guard levers acquired most of their fame from American cinema and the traditions they still embody, which gives them a special charm. These rifles can be cocked more quickly

Look out for certain "anemic" calibers in this range, just about adequate for roebuck.

The trigger-guard lever: a symbol of the "Wild West."

accused them of such faults as having a strong tendency to jam and being incapable of taking suitably powerful ammunition. The latter point was undoubtedly the most damaging.

Since about 1970, improvements in locking actions (mechanisms borrowing energy from gas and ammunition) have erased these faults. This system, similar to that of the smoothbore guns, can take anything from the .222 Rem. up to the muscular .338 Win. Mag. The semi-automatic has the advantage of an immediate follow-up shot to end the suffering of a wounded animal, but it could be misused by hunters who are excessively nostalgic for assault rifles, because it allows them to keep firing unnecessarily. For this reason, the semi-automatic is sometimes seen in a bad light and has sometimes even been banned from certain hunts in Europe. Semi-automatic

(and without coming down from the shoulder) than can the bolt actions. However, the slowness of loading and unloading can be annoying and hardly reassuring at all with the tubular magazine models. In addition, a fair number of these weapons use ammunition that is not powerful enough for hunting big game.

Any choice has to be made according to the available caliber.

Here, we can point to a number of makes:
– Marlin Caliber .444, and, for very short ranges, the .45–70 Gov.;
– Winchester (94) in Marlin Caliber .307, .356, .358, or .444;
– Browning (BLR) in Caliber .300 Win. Mag., .7 Rem., or .270 Win.;
– Savage (99) in Caliber .300 Savage.

SEMI-AUTOMATIC RIFLES

Semi-automatic rifles were invented around 1900. For a long time they aroused a certain distrust, as people

Ejector fort of a Remington semi-automatic, with sighting ramp.

Guns with Rifled Barrels

Regular maintenance is indispensable for avoiding jams.

rifles and pump action are prohibited in the UK.

The semi-automatic rifle has four principal faults:

– It has a "fishing rod" feel that comes from the unusual length of the breechcasing.

– It is slow and noisy to cock and chamber a cartridge.

– It is generally fairly heavy.

– Other hunters find it difficult to see whether the chamber and the breech are empty. This can sometimes cause concern, which is most unwelcome when relaxation and a good mood are desired. In the end, this rifle is only as good as its user. A responsible person will never overstep the limits of safety, and appropriate care for his weapon will keep it performing well and function-

ing perfectly. The pump rifle is similar in many respects to the semi-automatic rifle. It too can be cocked very rapidly, and reliability is 100 percent, because it is not dependent on pressures developed by the cartridge. Precision is theoretically a little better than that of the semi-automatic, but this is an asset which can still be undervalued by the inexperienced hunter.

RIFLES WITH BREAK OPEN ACTIONS

The Express

The Express emerged around 1860. It was named for the powerful, rapid steam locomotives of the day. Residents of many British colonies were very keen on hunting large and dangerous animals, and the Express

was tailored to the needs of dispatching a large-caliber bullet of a high kinetic energy at a relatively short range and getting in a second shot, if possible, without missing. The reliability of this rifle justifies the confidence that certain tropical hunting guides, who use it as a security weapon even today, have placed in it.

In more reasonable calibers, the Express has become the favorite weapon of the lover of covert shooting, over short and medium ranges under 100 m.

The term "gun" is equally justifiable for such a weapon that has remained typically European. This becomes evident when you consult American ammunition catalogs: none of the larger gunmakers produce a rim cartridge suitable for breechloading weapons. As far as we know, only the manufacturer A. Square makes them in small quantities.

Here are several good reasons to justify the considerable financial investment in an Express: it does not jam; the fall of the barrels makes for safe and easy loading; and it is very compact (in length of barrel it is clearly shorter than a bolt-action Mauser, for example). Another advantage is that sometimes a rifle barrel can be fitted to the action of a shotgun (often in 20 gauge). Finally, few gun lovers can resist a silhouette so characteristic that it summons the image of big-game hunting adorned with all its inherent fantasies.

On the other hand, the hunter cannot stray far from the type of ammunition which was used to regulate the rifle, if he wishes to shoot the best possible group. Moreover, the skilled craftmanship required to build an Express justifies a pretty high price for the so-called basic version.

Although too powerful for animals like roebuck, the old 9.3 x 74R still enjoys tremendous success.

Guns with Rifled Barrels

Kipplauf, "the winner": precision, lightness, safety, and elegance.

The Kipplauf one-shot breechloading rifle

The Kipplauf rifle's origins can be traced back to the end of the 19th century in Central Europe and England. Today, the Austrians and Germans are the principal producers of this type of rifle, which is quite often made and finished in a luxurious manner. This gun is about as far away as you can get from the semi-automatic.

This very lightweight and slight-looking weapon is really only to be considered if it is fitted with telescopic sights. This enables the purist hunter to practice stalking and approach in the context of selective firing, which is increasingly favored. Manual loading of the weapon allows the shooter to move with a cartridge in the chamber, without the risk of the gun going off accidentally. The hammer spring is very discreetly put under tension just before firing. Watch out, however, for this classic pitfall encountered by too-powerful ammunition: with such a light rifle, the shock to the system caused by an excessively brutal recoil can turn into a handicap, ending with a small advertisement in a specialist magazine to sell the rifle.

Too much power is actually a misnomer, since the real capability of this weapon lies in its capacity to place a single bullet very precisely in the lethal zone.

MIXED WEAPONS: SMOOTHBORE AND RIFLED BARRELS

This niche in the weapons market is occupied by two systems: the combination gun, equipped with one smoothbore barrel and one rifled; and the drilling, equipped with two side-by-side smoothbore barrels and a rifled barrel beneath. We will discuss only the latter configuration, as it is by far the more widespread system. This original idea of mixing two basically distinct categories of projectile was created in response to the desire for greater versatility on the part of hunters who are lucky enough to operate in a rich and varied environment. The drilling gun offers impressive firepower adequate for facing any situation at any given moment, be it big or small game.

All forms of versatile weapon suffer from the well-known paradox of not being very good for any one thing:

– The lack of balance inherent in the weight of the three barrels mitigates against rapid aiming, particularly up in the sky toward a fast-moving bird.

– Using a single-rifled barrel when hunting big game leaves no room for error, since the slugs from a smoothbore barrel cannot be relied on beyond 35–40 m or 38-43 yards (12 gauge).

– In urgent situations, the instinctive maneuver of the selective shooter as he chooses the appropriate trigger requires calm, *sang-froid*, and true mastery.

Because these few characteristics need deter nobody, large numbers of hunters have been committed to the drilling for a very long time.

The Express-drilling gun

The Express-drilling gun, just the opposite of the mixed weapon and not as well known, features two side-by-side rifled barrels above a single smoothbore tube. Generally regarded as a deluxe weapon, this gun has a lot of style, but it also suffers from a general lack of balance.

Attach a moderate weight to the end of your normal smoothbore gun, and bring it up to the shoulder. It will feel the same as if you were trying to raise an Express-

drilling gun. Pigeons and woodcock need not have any fear however: this gun is more for the big-game lover who wants to relieve his territory of a few surplus predators.

Let us conclude with a strange object, the Bock-drilling. This surprising combination of such different calibers is in fact equivalent to a mixed weapon to which a small-diameter rifled barrel has been added for shooting predators (or even roebuck). Regulating this combination of barrels is not easy. Only certain rifled calibers (large and small) are compatible within themselves and can provide the correct ballistic coincidence. Most of these powerful weapons come from the gunmaking town of Ferlach, in Austria.

The combination of "smooth and rifled" ensures that the shooter is not found wanting on land rich in diversity.

AMMUNITION FOR RIFLED BARRELS

There are 200 different calibers for shoulder arms on the market today. This is clearly far more than is needed: four or five would be enough to hunt all of the game that exists. However, market forces have encouraged many manufacturers to create their own special cartridges. You might sometimes find yourself with different makes of ammunition whose similarity can lead to confusion, so alike are they in external appearance. Three examples are: the 7 x 64 (Brenneke), the .270 (Winchester), and the .280 (Remington), whose ballistics are identical.

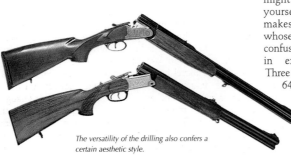

The versatility of the drilling also confers a certain aesthetic style.

Guns with Rifled Barrels

A small selection of current cartridges.

The range of caliber extends from the tiny .17 Remington (4.3 mm in diameter with a 1.6 g bullet) to the gigantic .700 Nitro Express (about 18 mm in diameter with a 64.8 g bullet).

In Europe, the manufacturer often gives the nominal caliber and then the length of the cartridge in mm, such as 7 x 64. The equivalent for break open action guns is the 7 x 65R. This last letter, in the context of "break-open" weapons, means "rim" in English or *Rand* in German, which is to say a rim on which the extractor can exert a sharp and powerful thrust:

– 8 x 68S (S = *Spitzer*) corresponds to the modernized German 8 mm (enlarged to 8.2 mm) and subsequently equipped with a pointed bullet.

– 8 x 57 JRS (J = I, for *Infanterie*) is the former German regulation ammunition (rimmed version).
– 7 x 66 SE (SE = Super Express). This high-capacity, high-muzzle velocity bullet (with tapering case),

Large-caliber bullet after expansion (note the groove marks).

created in about 1925, anticipating our present-day Magnums.

Magnums possess the particular feature of having a greater powder charge than that of standard cartridges (the case has an increased interior), and they are also equipped with a belted case. This rimless case does not have a rim to sit on the end of the chamber, but is supported by a belt used to facilitate opening the breech, avoiding the adverse effect of the high-pressure Magnum – the inextricable cartridge stuck in the chamber.

The Anglo-Saxon system

The Anglo-Saxon system uses the hundredth-of-an-inch measurement (1 inch = 25.4 mm) for Calibers 30 and 44, for example. More often, however, the

THE RECOIL EFFECT OF HUNTING WEAPONS

This physical phenomenon, well known to hunters, can become unpleasant and even unbearable beyond a certain measure. Recoil is a reaction that seeks dynamically to balance the energy needed to fire a projectile or projectiles. In other words, the pressure produced by the ignition of the powder acts on part on the projectile traveling forward along the barrel ("guided" in rifled weapons), and so on, in this sequence: on the cartridge case; on the head of the breechblock; on the lugs of the locking mechanism; on the housing of the breechblock (or the lumps of the barrel); on the stock; and, finally, on the shooter's shoulder. The physical laws of motion can give a theoretical value to the speed of the recoil and the kinetic energy, if the weight of the weapon is known (see table for a definition of kinetic energy).

If the mass of the weapon were identical to that of the bullet, each would travel at an identical speed. Include

Kinetic energy

Mass of weapon x speed of recoil =
Mass of bullet x starting velocity of bullet;
thus

$$\text{Speed of recoil} = \frac{\text{Mass of bullet} \quad x \quad \text{Starting velocity of bullet}}{\text{Mass of weapon}}$$

in this simple formula the mass of the powder and its speed of ejection (at about 1400 m/s), and you see that the missile effect of the release of gases at the barrel exit could amount to as much as 40 percent of the total recoil. Other factors also come into play, such as the forcing of the bullet along the barrel; the length of the forcing cone (the smooth part between the chamber and the start of the rifling); and the track of the grooves. The physical constitution of the shooter and the shape of the stock also contribute to the kind of feeling imparted, but these are impossible to evaluate numerically. The present custom of using weapons that are too light for the power of ammunition employed often exacts a high

price in the form of violent recoil with an insidiously deterrent effect. For that reason, do not exceed a charge of 30–32 g of lead with a smoothbore weighing 2.6 kg. Similarly, with a rifle loaded with a 9.3 x 62 (.366 Mauser), it would not be reasonable for the firearm to weigh less than 3.4 kg. The popularization of ballistic tables can no doubt give rise to a certain false knowledge, directing people in a systematic way to make poor choices about super performance. Logic must be applied: accept a compromise between the weight of weapon and the power of ammunition.

Guns with Rifled Barrels

THE BALLISTIC CHARACTERISTICS OF A CARTRIDGE FOR A RIFLED WEAPON

We do not have space here to describe the performance of the ammunition used according to the size and the resistance of the game being hunted. Such documentation is generally available from distributors and importers.

Waiting like this, a hunter is no longer giving much thought to ballistics.

Taking the example of a very well-known type, this is what can be found:

Maker: RWS-Dynamit-Nobel (Germany).

Caliber: .300 Winchester Magnum.

Type of bullet: TUG 11.7 g. This is a double-core bullet in which the rear part is hard and assures penetration, while the front part is softer and guarantees expansion on impact.

The weight is 11.7 g, or in grains:

$$\frac{11.7}{0.0648} = 180 \text{ grains}$$

The back end is lightly pointed into the shape of a torpedo (TUG = *Torpedo Universal Geschoss*) in order to lighten the drag, an aerodynamic component detrimental to the stability and speed of the projectile in flight.

Use: red deer, wild boar, etc.

Maximum gas pressure: 3900 bars (about 3900 kg/cm²).

Length of barrel used: 650 mm.

Velocity: given in meters per second (m/s) at 0.50, 100, 200, and 300 m.

Such a huge choice at least gives hunters plenty to talk about.

Kinetic energy: given in joules for the same distances detailed above.
$Ec = 1/2\ mv^2$
m = mass of bullet in kg.
v = velocity of bullet in m/s.
To obtain the equivalents in kg, divide by 9.81.

The flight path: This indicates the trajectory, the extent of its curve, and how far it is vertically above or below the line of sight. These factors have been worked out in terms of a range adjustment clearly indicated in the document.

Zeroing:
This process ensured that the rifle's sights are adjusted to the proper point of impact.

Ideally, the rifle should be zeroed so that the bullet strikes the line of sight twice. The hunting industry has devised a standard adjustment to give the shooter a deviation of no more than 4 cm, which should be accurate enough to have a good chance of striking within the lethal zone. It is therefore not necessary to make any corrections within 20 to 40 m of the zeroed range. The flight paths corresponding to the zeroed range are extremely useful, as they allow adjustments to be made when lacking sufficient range. According to the table, our .300 should be aimed up 4

cm from a 100 m setting to zero in at 195 m. Hunters who care about their own performance and that of their weapons should be capable of carrying out this operation by themselves, rather than entrusting it to a gunsmith (even a good one, since his eyesight may be different).

Guns with Rifled Barrels

thousandth-of-an-inch measurement is used: .222 Remington, .300 Winchester Magnum, .375 H&H, and .416 Rigby. For example, 222 x 0.0254 mm = 5.6 mm.

Here are more examples:
– .470 NE (NE = Nitro Express). These cartridges for the English Express rifle are loaded with modern smokeless powder (nitro), as opposed to the older black powder.

An excellent caliber, though not very common.

– .30–36. Caliber 30 ammunition was designed in 1906 (for the Springfield rifle).
– .45–70. Caliber 45 ammunition was formerly loaded with 70 grains of black powder (1 grain = 0.0648 g), with the same applying to the famous .30–30.
– .22–250 Remington. Remington designed the ammunition on the basis of the .250 Savage adjusted for .22 caliber. This is the same type as the popular "wildcat cartridge" modified for a reload.

Telescopic sights are indispensable for checking out the ground (and for the approach).

Between the flint knife of the first Homo sapiens and the all-weather rifle with its composite stock lie 35,000 years of experience and evolution, guided first of all by need and later by a hunter's passion.

The call to start the battue has just been sounded.

Guns with Rifled Barrels

Here is a table for adapting caliber according to the game being hunted. Please remember that the match-ups provided are only indications and do not claim to be official or exhaustive. Also do not forget that legislation varies according to country, both for ammunition and for the species that may be hunted.

AMMUNITION SUITABLE FOR USE WITH SOME KINDS OF GAME ANIMALS

Animals hunted	Suitable ammunition
Elephant, buffalo, hippopotamus	.460 Weatherby, .458 Winchester Magnum, .470 NE, .416 Rigby, .500 NE, .500 A. Square, .416 Remington Magnum, .375 H&H, .378 Weatherby, 10.75 x 73, 9.3 x 64, .505 Gibbs
Large bear, large antelope, big cats, large deer, wapiti, moose, caribou	.375 H&H, .338 Winchester Magnum, .338 Lapua Mag., .358 Norma Mag., .340 Weatherby Mag., 8 x 68S, 8 mm Rem. Mag., .308 Norma Mag., 9.3 x 62, 9.3 x 64, 9.3 x 74R
Wild boar, red deer, fallow deer, Virginia deer, black bear, reindeer	30.06 Spr., .280 Rem., 7 mm Rem. Mag., 7 x 66 SE, 7 x 64, 93 x 62, 7 x 65R, 7 x 57R, .284 Winchester, 8 x 57 JS (or JRS), .308 Win., .300 Win. Mag., .30 R Blaser, .300 H&H
Moufflon, chamois, ibex, Rocky Mountain goat, Dall sheep	.270 Win., .280 Rem., .284 Win., .7–08 Rem., .308 Win., .264 Win. Mag., .25–06, 6–5 x 57R, .260 Rem. Mag., .243 Win., 7 x 64, 7 x 65R, 7 x 57R, .7 Rem. Mag., 6 x 62R Frères, 6 mm Rem., 6–5 x 65 RWS
Roebuck	.243 Win., .270 Win., 7 x 57R, 7 x 64, 7 x 65R, 6–5 x 57R, 6 x 62, .22–50 Rem., .25–06, 5–6 x 57, .222 Rem., 5–6 x 50R Mag., 5–6 x 52R
Fox	.22 Hornet, .222 Rem., 5–6 x 50R Mag., .22–250 Rem., .220 Swift, .22 Mag. (rimfire)
Small game, crow, etc.	.22 Hornet, .17 Rem. (rimfire), .22 LR

A range of large-caliber cartridges that would have pleased Ernest Hemingway.

The firearm is the child of the oldest industry in the history of mankind. Because of this, the gun or rifle that the hunter uses is never a mere instrument, whatever it may have cost. A highly symbolic value is attached. The techniques of hunting have been refined, and its armory has become all the richer in its diversity, technology, and *savoir-faire*. Bear this in mind as you get to know and learn how to choose your weapons. At the same time, keep a special place for the unmixed pleasure of making an irrational choice – in other words, when it is love at first sight.

For the "very large game": from the .600 to the 9.3 x 64.

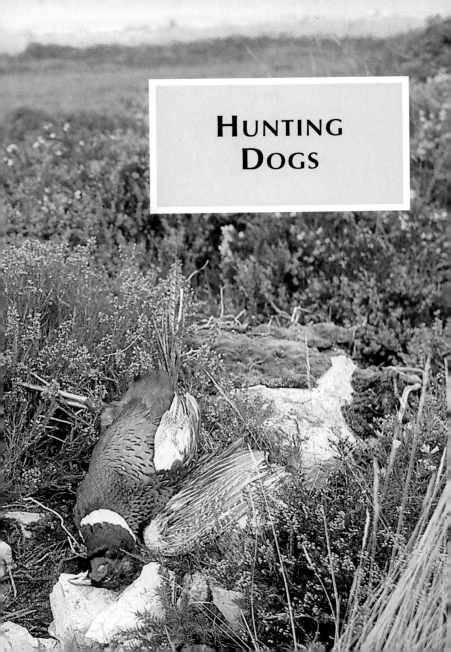

HUNTING
DOGS

Health

Because they are out and about in all types of weather, hunting dogs are particularly exposed to serious risk from parasites and infection.

Fortunately, sicknesses of a viral or bacterial origin can be avoided thanks to vaccines, and existing medicines can successfully combat both internal and external parasites. Depending on the animal and the epidemiological situation of the country, the veterinarian responsible has time to determine the choice of vaccination program and preventive treatments against parasites.

PARASITES

The most common external parasites are ticks, mites, and fleas. Not only do they directly affect the health of the dog, they may also become carriers of other parasites or diseases. We know, for example, that fleas are crucial to the transmission of tapeworms and that ticks are the carriers of piroplasmosis. The most common internal parasites are the roundworm and the tapeworm or flatworm.

INFECTIOUS DISEASES
Canine distemper

Canine distemper, a contagious disease that mostly affects puppies, has long been feared by breeders. The first symptoms are generally coughing, conjunctivitis (or pinkeye), and vomiting. Nerve problems can set in later, especially in adult dogs, with symptoms affecting the lungs, the gastrointestinal system, and the skin. These can ultimately lead to the animal's death. The primary vaccination for distemper is given to puppies from the age of two months, with the first booster given one month later.

Brucellosis

Brucellosis is a very contagious form of viral gastroenteritis. Although it affects dogs of all ages, it chiefly affects puppies from 6–12 weeks old and can lead to a very high death rate. The symptoms include fever, vomiting, a foul-smelling form of hemorrhagic diarrhea, and dehydration. This

Even before weaning, the puppy must be wormed.

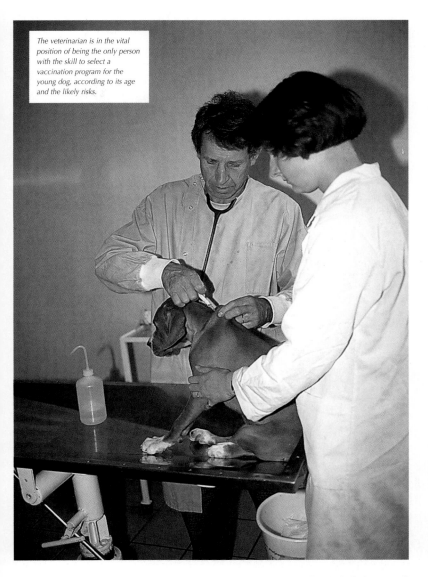

The veterinarian is in the vital position of being the only person with the skill to select a vaccination program for the young dog, according to its age and the likely risks.

condition can cause rapid death for infected animals. The vaccination program for brucellosis is the same as for canine distemper.

Rubarth's hepatitis

Rubarth's hepatitis is the canine version of viral hepatitis. It is frequently seen in puppies, and its symptoms include a high temperature, gastroenteritis, and sometimes conjunctivitis. It is not transmittable to humans. This disease is rarely fatal, with the infected animal usually recovering in a few days. The timing of vaccinations for Rubarth's is the same as for canine distemper and brucellosis.

Leptospirosis

Leptospirosis is a contagious disease caused by bacteria transmitted through contact with the urine of contaminated rats or through the ingestion of water tainted with this urine. Symptoms include hepatic and stomach upset with vomiting and hemorrhagic diarrhea, as well as kidney problems complicated by jaundice. While rats are the primary carriers of leptospirosis, any dog that has contracted it can become a carrier and can transmit the disease for several years. It is therefore necessary to vaccinate the puppy at about three months of age, and in addition to give an annual booster (sometimes twice a year in areas at risk).

Piroplasmosis

Piroplasmosis, transmitted by ticks, causes progressive destruction of the red corpuscles, leading to an anemic condition in the dog. The dog's urine becomes dark and may contain blood. If the disease is caught in time, a good veterinarian should be able to cure the dog, and there is now an effective vaccine available.

Kennel cough

Kennel cough, a very contagious viral respiratory disease that is rampant in kennels and breeding establishments, can be fatal. The primary vaccination for kennel cough can be given at two months of age, with a booster one month later, and then it should be repeated annually.

Rabies

Rabies is the only disease subject to international regulation in regard to vaccination. Transmission of this virus can result from biting, licking, or a claw wound. The disease takes two forms in dogs. The first

Nature is full of traps, like these ticks that are carriers of piroplasmosis.

LIST OF THE DOG'S PHYSIOLOGICAL CHARACTERISTICS

Temperature (rectal): 100.4°–102.2°F (38°–39°C).

Breathing frequency: 10–40 breaths per minute.

Pulse: 70–160 beats per minute for an adult dog, and up to 200–220 bpm for a puppy.

Average age of puberty: 7–10 months for a male, and 6–12 months for a female.

Female ovulation (heat) frequency: generally twice a year, for an average of 12–21 days.

Best period for mating: between the ninth and thirteenth days of heat.

Gestation: 57–63 days.

The hunting dog is exposed to all sorts of risks from parasites and infections, and must be subject to a rigorous health care routine.

form, known as "furious rabies," is fairly rare, fortunately – the infected animal becomes aggressive, slavers, swallows painfully, and usually dies a few days after the appearance of symptoms. In the other form, known as "dumb rabies," a variety of symptoms may be observed: gastroenteritis, trembling, and a paralysis that begins with the rear limbs.

The paralysis later reaches the jaws, but the animal does not become aggressive. This is the most common form of canine rabies, and it can also be very dangerous to humans because it cannot always be diagnosed immediately. In areas most at risk, every dog suffering from neurological problems that cannot be precisely diagnosed must be suspected of being rabid.

Feeding

The hunting dog is a true athlete, and a strict and responsible check on its diet is essential to maintain good shape and good health.

Today, dogs are fed largely on dried foods.

FEEDING HABITS

A dog's feeding habits are established at the weaning stage. This is the time to get the puppy used to the foods that it will consume later. The transition from a milk diet to eating solid foods must be carried out over a period of at least three weeks, from the age of three or four weeks. This progressive dietary transition is aimed at preventing attacks of diarrhea and preparing the digestive enzymes for new foods. This type of diet is a lot easier to organize because the puppy will eat three meals a day.

Once the dog is mature, it should be fed only once a day, preferably in the evening so that it can digest its meal calmly during sleep. The diet must be balanced and geared to the needs of an animal, not to the tastes of a human (despite the fact that, for thousands of years, dogs were fed with scraps from the master's table). Of course, the traditional food prepared at home is still used today, constituting the diet of about one in every two dogs. However, to provide a correctly balanced meal, we need to understand the needs of our dogs and the nutritional value of the primary ingredients used, and this requires both discipline and knowledge. In fact, the composition of the food should be varied according to the dog's condition, taking into account such dietary behavior as how it eats the food, how it chews it, and how often and how much it eats at each meal.

A RAPID EVOLUTION

Meat as dog food was not regularly recommended until the middle of the 19th century, and it was only during the 20th century that the canine diet gradually became more balanced, thanks to the introduction

A puppy must be fed three times a day.

The physical prowess of a good hunting dog depend upon a balanced diet.

Feeding

A litter of puppies must be given meals according to a regular schedule.

of green vegetables, powdered bone, and cod-liver oil. After World War II, dog-food manufacturers began focusing on balanced diets, geared to the actual dietary needs of dogs, and which also happened to be easier to stock. Research into canine diet has helped establish rules for a rational diet. The best solution for feeding your dog lies with using foods manufactured by professionals according to appropriate methods.

AN EASIER-TO-MANAGE DIET

Pet-food manufacturers follow international standards that determine the amount of calories, protein, fat, carbohydrates, vitamins, minerals, and trace elements required to meet pets' dietary needs. Moreover, the results of research carried out in veterinary schools and the manufacturers' own laboratories make it possible to develop foods suited to the different physiological states that occur during the life of a dog: growth, upkeep, work, gestation, and suckling. Commercially prepared foods are much easier to use and also guarantee digestive stability for the dog. These are also more

A good diet makes a dog easier to train.

economical than homemade meals, particularly for feeding big dogs or several dogs at a time. On a practical level, mashed or chunky food in cans is generally less concentrated and therefore less nourishing than biscuit-type and other dried forms. On average, you need three times more moist food than dried food to satisfy the same dog's hunger. However, it is important to remember that an animal eating dried food needs a permanent supply of water. In addition, the dog's stool has a better consistency, is less frequent, and is less odorous with a dry diet.

Cans are easy to stock and transport, and they can be used to supplement food prepared at home.

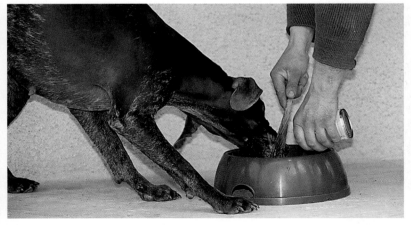

Training

Training a dog to hunt is part of the duties of the hunter, but it is also one of the pleasures. It is important to use good methods for all events.

A well-trained dog is a guarantee of success in hunting.

Whatever the individual hunter's experience, the training of a hunting dog is an essential procedure. Training is the act that enables the dog to transform its animal instinct into a way of working; in other words, to focus its natural behavior and enhance the functioning in the field. Even if this labor of love and patience does not result in perfection, it will lead to a long-lasting partnership.

KNOWLEDGE THAT CANNOT BE IGNORED

During hunting practice, it is best to avoid giving lessons that are too intensive. You must give the dog ample time to assimilate each stage of its training before passing on to the next. Remember that it is possible to set up a certain program but not a specific timetable. The first important stage is to gain the dog's trust and subsequently avoid betraying it. Each exercise must be expressed with a few simple words and key gestures. Don't ever forget that the dog understands only the terms it is taught, and remember that it is absolutely useless, and quite harmful, to let yourself get angry. The animal will become disorientated and will remember only your angry body language. The commands you use can be expressed in different ways: by word, by gesture and whistle, or by horn when the hunt is on. In the beginning, gestures and words should be enough. It is essential that your tone of voice and body movements work together in harmony, as much when you are being gentle as when you are being firm. To be precise, a command must be as brief as possible, and the words used must always be the same.

Today, there are increasing numbers of professional trainers.

Obedience is always the key to training and to a good level of efficiency.

Training

Training forges a strong relationship between the hunter and his future partner.

AN IRON FIST IN A VELVET GLOVE

Rewards are a major tool in training. Generally given in the form of a tidbit, a reward should be combined with a pat and a few words of praise.

They should not be overdone, however: if the dog deserves several rewards at one time, it is better to discontinue that particular lesson and return to it later than to stuff the dog with tidbits. Another important element of training is punishment, which should be given only when the dog refuses to carry out an exercise it knows very well. Punishment should never be used to make a dog perform a command or try to make it

understand something. In every case, the punishment must be brief and moderate. With some sensitive animals, a strong rebuff or a simpler form of punishment can be used.

Don't forget about the secondary effects of punishment. For example, if you confine your dog to a kennel to punish it, there is a strong chance that this place will become a "mental prison." This must be avoided at all costs.

A FEELING WHICH VARIES ACCORDING TO BREED

Whatever the breed, training a dog to hunt rarely

For some specialized hunts, a specific form of training makes all the difference.

Sometimes a few clever tricks can aid in the dog's education, such as this device for laying a trail.

produces specific problems. However, you must be aware enough not to make mistakes that could cause the dog to develop serious and sometimes irreversible faults. The most delicate concept of training is to be sensitive to what the tasks should really be. In fact, it is impossible to think of beginning any aspect of training without having determined the precise goal in advance. Making this decision is often made easier when you consider the natural aptitudes of certain breeds. In every case, the golden rule is to train the animal as often as possible within natural situations. "Theoretical learning" can never take the place of practice.

Correct training ensures that the dog will be easier to work with.

Terriers and Dachshunds

Terriers and dachshunds are small breeds but make very versatile hunters.

Most breeds of terrier originated in Britain. Some have become pets by virtue of their small size and the way they are groomed. However, this has not prevented the main breeds from remaining dedicated to hunting, which they do with an almost diabolical passion. The true leader of this group has always been the fox terrier, which comes in two types: smooth-haired and wirehaired. This is a determined little dog that owes its forceful temperament to having been bred to

hunt burrowing animals. Faithful, courageous, and intelligent, the fox terrier exercises its talents in numerous forms of hunting, and it sometimes even disrupts the established order among hunting dogs.

THE FOX KING

There are numerous descendants of Grand Champions to assure the hunter of finding a good partner for underground hunting. There is also no doubt that for this kind of hunting, the terrier can make best use of its powerful nose. Even if the prey being tracked to the tunnel (fox, badger, or nutria) leaves a relatively

strong trail, the difficulty really comes from the dog's having to work in burrows which the prey is constantly traversing. Since the master cannot always intervene quickly, the dog's intelligence and spirit of initiative must enable it to combine daring and wisdom in every situation.

Above ground, the jobs entrusted to terriers vary greatly. The most classic of these is still that of tracking big game in a battue. At such times, it becomes an excellent companion for a landowner in charge of small acreage. Whether employed in small numbers or in a true pack, the terrier locates the game and pursues it for a few minutes,

Terriers and dachshunds are small, versatile dogs that are at home in every situation.

Terriers, like this Jagd terrier and Jack Russell, can be found all over the world, hunting both big and small game.

meanwhile offering itself to a line of hunters waiting in position.

POPULAR TERRIERS IN GERMANIC LANDS

Other types of terrier are also highly regarded for hunting. Of these, the numbers of Jack Russell and Welsh terriers are increasing. The Germans, great specialists in big-game hunting, have also created a terrier intended for similar work: the *Jagd* (Hunt) terrier. Very similar to the fox terrier, the *Jagd* can be easily distinguished by its black-and-tan coat. This is an excellent dog for unearthing game and for the battue, to which it has been introduced by large numbers of hunters around the world. Its qualities are fairly similar to those

of the fox terrier, but generally it is even more spirited. Among terriers, the exception that confirms the rule is the Airedale. This is actually the only large terrier, reaching up to 23.5 inches (60 cm) in the

shoulders. Even though it actually is rarely used for hunting, it remains nonetheless a good dog for big game.

DACHSHUNDS: A FAMOUS SILHOUETTE

The other large group of small hunting dogs is the dachshund. This is the only breed in the world that constitutes a complete canine family. Doubtless they owe this privilege both to their famous silhouette, elongated and close to the ground, and to their versatile qualities. There are three sizes of dachshund and three types of coat, making a total of nine varieties. Their origins are undoubtedly very old, stemming from Germanic hunting methods, and more specifically from selective

The wirehaired fox terrier is a great partner to have for a demanding day's hunting.

Terriers and Dachshunds

Less widely known among hunters, the longhaired dachshund is nonetheless an excellent hunting dog.

breeding that has been very rigorous and thorough. Dachshunds are skilled helpers in the undergrowth, good beaters who bay well and are sufficiently slow not to disturb the game prematurely. They are equally good at scenting wounded big game. In addition, dachshunds have always been used for unearthing badgers and foxes, although this is not the activity that made them popular. However, they do owe their breed name to it, since the word "dachshund" means "badger hound."

The smallest of the great specialists

The original type of dachshund is the short-haired dog, which has descended from a large family of brown-coated hounds common in the Ardennes and throughout the Alpine region (another modern survivor is the Alpine basset, found in Austria). The longhaired variety appeared later as a result of crossbreeding with small spaniels. Not until the 19th century did the smooth-haired variety come into being, after crossing with British terriers. There is only one standard for all dachshunds. It was created in 1925 by the German Breeders Club and was permanently adopted by the International Hunting Federation (IHF) in 1947.

On the ground, dachshunds display a great variety of capabilities. This breed possesses a solid reputation as a scent hound. In Western Europe, the skill in sniffing out wounded big game has increased the breed's fame. This is far from being the only talent, however; the qualities of tracking, working in the undergrowth, and possessing great energy are appreciated in woodland areas, when the dog is either solo or in a small pack. With equal skill, they seek out game from the smallest to the biggest, which they flush and drive toward the hunter. As burrowing dogs, they are used for hunting badgers and foxes underground. They are currently used more often when "turfing out" foxes pulled to the mouth of the holes. The variety most widely found among hunt-

The smooth-haired is the original variation in the great dachshund family.

ers remains the wirehaired, although you may easily come across a few smooth-hairs and even, more rarely, some longhairs.

Not all dachshunds are devoted to the pleasures of the hunt. However, we must still admire the way this dog has been selectively bred, based on natural aptitude tests that serve as a model for the kind.

Nordic and Original Dogs

In addition to their form, their hunting technique has remained fairly undeveloped.

With their characteristically pricked ears, Nordic and original dogs originate from countries where hunting was practiced in extreme conditions. Furthermore, this type has been preserved by the isolation of the lands in which they exist. You might encounter them in the southernmost regions of Europe, the Scandinavian countries or Siberia.

THE ELKHOUND

The elkhound is the most common of the Nordic dogs, tracing its origins back to the Vikings. This dog, with a compact and relatively short body, hunts big game, elk, and bear. It has a long, thick, rough coat, with a woolly undercoat that helps it withstand the harshest climates. The elkhound's furry mane acts as a muffler and gives it a unique appearance. The originality and authenticity of this breed are reasons for its early recognition in the world of dogs. Since the end of the 19th century, the elkhound has enjoyed a keen success in many countries, such as in the United States, where it is much admired.

A redoubtable efficiency

On the hunting ground, the elkhound's strong nose enables it to track game in almost unbelievable situations. Its endurance and courage then take over when it must keep a large animal steadily at bay while waiting for the hunter to

The elk is highly coveted by Northern hunters.

arrive. The ringing, repetitive bark is fearsomely effective. In action, it is a good partner, but it is not a submissive dog. It has managed to retain its sense and spirit of enterprise.

The elkhound's shape is well adapted to mountainous regions, so it is at home in thick, coniferous forests rising from rocky ground. There are several varieties of elkhound that can be linked to the Siberian laïka, due to their similar forms and hunting styles. The Karelian bearhound is a remarkable bear hunter. Also used for other kinds of hunts, such as elk in Scandinavia or wild boar in Central Europe, it has hunting in its blood and naturally shows great sensitivity.

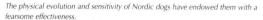

The physical evolution and sensitivity of Nordic dogs have endowed them with a fearsome effectiveness.

As its name suggests, the Karelian bearhound is a specialist hunter of these animals, while also being an excellent dog for other game, such as elk or wild boar.

Nordic and Original Dogs

The Portuguese podengo is a very versatile and active dog.

THE IBIZAN HOUND AND THE PODENGO

Another large family of hunting dogs with pricked ears is represented by the Ibizan hound (or Spanish podenco) and the Portuguese podengo. Along with the giant breeds, they make up the famous packs used in Iberian hunting. These breeds are probably of African origin, linked to the greyhounds. Although they have an elegant silhouette, slender and lean, their necks are shorter and their heads are more massive than those of the greyhound.

Elegant and spirited hunters

It is mainly in the manner of hunting that the Ibizan hound and the podengo stand out. Unlike the greyhound, they hunt with their noses to flush or pursue game. They cannot operate on high ground, like hounds can. Another special characteristic is that these dogs give voice only when the game is in sight. The most surprising thing about them is the peculiar way that they bound along rather than run, always looking for game. This way of moving enables them to see over the thick, rough vegetation of the countries in which they live, to spot fleeing game and so gain time in the chase. Mobile, pricked ears allow them to detect the slightest tremble in a thicket, and their noses help fix the location of game.

At home with all types of game

Traditionally used for hunting rabbit, the Ibizan hound and podengo are equally prized for big-game hunting. At most big hunts, which can bring together more than a hundred dogs, about half of the dogs are Ibizan hounds in Spain and podengos in Portugal. It is

Bred in arid countries, Ibizan hounds and podengos can tolerate the hunt under a fierce sun.

worth noting that, while Ibizan hounds have only two types of coat, Portuguese podengos have two types of coat as well as three different sizes: small, medium, and large. This

makes it easier to find a dog best suited to the kind of hunting and the ground available.

Associated with the mastiffs and used in important hunts, the big podengos specialize in hunting.

Hounds

A living expression of centuries of tradition, these breeds make up the largest number of hunting dogs.

The Swiss hound is a true jewel of a scent hound.

Specific to the hound is its solo use in the countries of Northern, Central and Eastern Europe, and North America, while in Western and Southern Europe it is also used in packs (sometimes consisting of nearly a hundred dogs). For these dogs, which characteristically pursue game by scent while giving voice, France is the principal country, boasting 27 breeds. The epitome of the hound nevertheless remains the St. Hubert, the only Belgian breed, yet the one recognized as the ancestor of all other current species. Among the modern dogs, the world's most widespread breed is the beagle. This small dog, so full of good qualities, owes its popularity to a compact size added to an inextinguishable love of hunting. Its origins are very old, and it probably has not always looked like it does today. The official standard has been registered by the Kennel club and was approved in 1987.

THE BEAGLE: AN ALMOST UNIVERSAL HUNTER

When out hunting, the beagle bustles about industriously but is never sloppy. It is very attentive and proves itself to be skilled in approach work. The traditional use for this breed is still hunting hare, and it is bred specifically for that sport. Thanks to its many talents, it is suitable for all kinds of game animals and works equally well alone or in a large pack. Beagles are used along with other

The beagle is the smallest of the hounds and it is also the most common.

breeds against fox, roebuck, and wild boar, and they will not refrain from diving into a thicket or thorn bush. For rabbit hunting, the beagle's small frame is an irreplaceable bonus. It nips into the undergrowth with a rare vigor. Blessed with real courage, this breed is very robust. The beagle is a quick mover, and it has a good nose and a voice that is sometimes a bit husky but is at the same time warm and rich. It is a fiercely effective hitter that could very well suit both the ardent novice

The Gascon griffon is a very enterprising and courageous dog.

and the seasoned veteran who appreciates a spirit of initiative. A strong character contributes to its popularity, and its docility is additionally pleasing.

THE GASCON BLUE: A FINE NOSE AND A GOOD VOICE

Of the many French breeds, the Gascon blues constitute the most complete family of hounds that exists. They are also the most noted outside of their country of origin for their distinctive noses and voices. It is this breed which has best maintained its original character (from the very beginning it possessed the essential qualities of a good hound). There are written records of blues going back to the 14th century. Subsequently, you can find continuous traces of the breed up to the present day. However, it was just in the 19th century that certain hunters utilized a more rigorous breeding program that gave the various Gascon blues their present form, with a greater regularity in bone

construction and a certain strengthening of the tissues. This was particularly true of the large blue, which assumed the role of patriarch of the Gascon breeds.

Potential bloodhounds

The large blue clings to the ground, as much in love with scenting as with hunting. Its complete con-

This Gascon epitomizes the qualities of nose and voice found in the large French hounds.

centration can lead it to make certain mistakes, distracting it from its surroundings and making some people think that it only obeys its instincts. However, the Gascon blue is actually a great specialist in delicate pursuit. When it

Hounds

Much used for battues, the basset griffon Vendéen is a keen worker in thorn bushes.

gets wind of a scent, it howls and raises its head. While seeking game, it sometimes freezes in this pose. On the trail, it can cover 33–49 feet (10–15 m), head raised and "trumpeting" into the wind, before getting its nose back on the ground to be sure it is on the right trail and starting off again. This is a very persistent and enterprising hound, and above all a dog for hares, although it can happily be used for other types of game.

It is worth noting that the Gascon blue is the only hound to have four varieties: a large dog, a medium-sized one, a basset, and a

griffon that delights lovers of thick-coated dogs.

FROM BASSETS TO LARGE PACK HUNTERS

The pack hunter breeds have a unique genetic heritage. They qualify as pack hunter dogs by virtue of their sense of discipline and pack spirit, and they are used almost exclusively for hunting big game, which remains a French specialty. Although this form of use may seem limited, these dogs number more than 20,000.

The bassets make up an important group. Their low stature, which bears the scientific name "achon-

droplasia," was originally a mutation affecting the skeletons of certain dogs. Breeders then genetically cultivated this phenomenon to create a type of hound that was closer to the ground and better suited to certain functions. This is the reason that bassets always appear to be a reduced version of a medium-sized or large breed, even though the maternal breed has more or less disappeared today. From a historical perspective, it is mainly with the development of hunting with guns that the situation with bassets has been knocked off balance. From the end of the 19th

The dachshunds are vigorous dogs with a familiar elongated silhouette.

century, each region with a family of hounds has also had a basset form. Although certain breeds have a standard dating from the early 1900s, the present lineage was fixed only after World War II. Today, the nomenclature of the IHF recognizes eight breeds of basset, of which five are French. There is the West-phalian basset of Germany, the Alpine basset in Austria, the Artois-Norman basset, the Gascon blue, the Brittany tawny, the large and petite basset griffon Vendéen of France, and the basset hound of Great Britain. This type of low-built hound also includes some breeds, such as the Swedish drever, who are not actually called bassets but whose shapes link them to this form.

Suitable for both big and small game

In the hunting field, the basset often becomes the helper of a hunter who wants just the basics and appreciates the breed's lesser speed and sharp, enterprising spirit. Bassets behave like all of the other hounds, giving loud voice during the pursuit of the game, but their movements are slower than those of their bigger fellows.

They are generally stereotyped as being better in the undergrowth, capable of flushing all kinds of game and giving the hunter only optimal shooting opportunities. In fact, things are not so simple, and it is a pity that they are stuck with this caricature, because they deserve a closer look. To avoid discussing only the best-known and most wide-spread breeds, we will point out that the British basset hound and the large basset griffon Vendéen were creat-ed to hunt hare, a skill which requires a certain number of qualities. Today, you can still come across a few rabbit-hunting outfits that successfully use excel-lent teams of bassets.

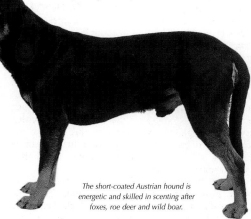

The short-coated Austrian hound is energetic and skilled in scenting after foxes, roe deer and wild boar.

Hounds

In addition, the Artois-Norman and the Gascon blue basset are, in their hunting styles, more suited to hunting hare. It is essential to know the origins of the different species of basset and their methods of hunting before heading off into the country and asking a dog to do something that it has not been bred to do.

BLOODHOUNDS: THEIR WORTH IS RISING

The name "bloodhound" refers to hounds that specialize in scenting out the blood of wounded big game, not the blood-

The Jura bruno had a big hand in the "modernization" of the old Swiss breeds.

red color of their coats. Highly specialized hounds of German origin, the Bavarian and Hanoverian bloodhounds are slowly but surely being introduced into regions where hunters wish to seek wounded big game. These dogs owe this position to rigorous genetic breeding that predestines them to a precise function. It is true that there is nothing new in this sport, for in a 1379 manuscript there are valuable pieces of advice given in the chapters on archery. The treatises on hunting of Feyerabendt (1582), Flemming (1719), Doebel (1746), and Von Heppe (1751) include substantial chapters detailing the use of bloodhounds. All of the dogs described were

of medium build yet fairly massive, with solid bones. They had large muzzles and heads, with pendent, kidney-shaped ears, and they worked with their noses glued to the ground. Today's Hanoverian bloodhound, the older of the two German species of bloodhound, is very similar to this. The Bavarian variety was not actually created until the beginning of the 19th century, by hunters in the Bavarian and Tyrolean Alps. They wanted a lighter version than the Hanoverian and so crossed it with Austrian dogs, notably the brandelbracke and the Tyrolean pointer. The new breed then took the name "Bavarian bloodhound." Its club was founded in 1919, and from 1930, the Germans, Austrians, and Hungarians united to form the International Union of Bloodhound Clubs.

An expert worker

In practice, the Bavarian bloodhound has the reputation of being a little more lively than its cousin from Hanover. It nonetheless possesses all of the specific qualities of a good bloodhound, with a reflective, steady, and very

The pack hunters, descendants of the great hunting traditions of France, make up a hunting heritage that is unique in the world.

courage in case it must hunt and take down a large, wounded animal. Everything about this dog indicates that, on the physical level, it is cut out for rough duties. It has strong bone structure and a deep rib cage. A large nose is foremost among this breed's virtues, and its powerful voice is always surprising when it is not working on a lead. It has a good temperament and displays devotion. It has the serious air of an individual with keen concentration, ready to fulfill an important or delicate assignment. However, we cannot advise just any hunter who is tempted to follow blood trails to buy such a dog, as it takes three to four years and a lot of discipline to train one and form a truly operational team.

well-balanced character. It is a basic requirement in locating wounded game that the dog does not yield to its instincts and bolt off on the trail of a fresh or unwounded animal, even if it crosses the path of or goes bounding past the dog. Nor must the dog take off from the shooting position and then lose the trail at the first serious snag. A game trail can be very long, especially with wild boar. Like any good hunting dog, the bloodhound must pursue the trail with calmness and *sang-froid* and conserve its energy. The Bavarian dog has this quiet power, an Olympian calm, added to extreme tenacity and a good spirit of initiative to thwart the ruses of the animal being tracked. It must have

Pointers, Setters, and Spaniels

Chiefly used for hunting game birds, pointers are either versatile or specialist dogs.

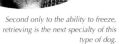

The growth in the number of hunters living in urban areas, something that is intimately linked to the problem of rural depopulation, has acted in favor of the pointers. This breed's special skill is to indicate the presence of game by freezing on the spot, enabling the hunter to fire from a good range. In some countries, the practice of people releasing game (mainly pheasants) over the generations has played a large part in the breed's development. However, this practice is diminishing, even though the actual number of pointers seems stable. Many owners are turning toward field trial competitions.

Second only to the ability to freeze, retrieving is the next specialty of this type of dog.

Others prefer the "natural source" of migrating birds, notably woodcock. Competitions regularly show

The Irish setter is one of the best pointing dogs for use in wetlands.

A more powerful dog, the Gordon setter is seen here in fairly mountainous territory.

a large span of breeds among the top-placed dogs: pointer, setter, German pointer, the incomparable Brittany spaniel, and sometimes the Korthals griffon.

SETTERS AND POINTERS

In the hunting field, pointers and English setters occupy a place apart. That there are different classes for the Continentals and the British is not a matter of chance. These pointers assumed their present form at the end of the 19th century, and in the course of breeding have become like precision machines, devilishly efficient. Endowed with great physical abilities and a

rapid, strong, and loose galloping run, they are wide-ranging hunters with genial temperaments. They also have the most powerful noses in the world of dogs. Unfortunately, the very selection of qualities that makes them shine in field trials can sometimes betray them. The image of these dogs as great for hunting trials makes them the object of a trite observation: They are impossible to keep under control, can be only used in wide-open spaces, hunt too quickly, and go too far – in short, they are useless for practical hunting. In fact, they are quite the opposite, very well suited to hunting in

today's conditions, with wild game having become rare and difficult to contain. In this context, high-power dogs clearly have a much better chance of succeeding than do their fellows.

True artists
These dogs are capable of taking any risk, often hunting on a razor-edge, moving toward the scent with authority, and cordoning off the area even in foul weather. The pride of a hunter (who is not always capable of appreciating such a situation) can often turn him against his dog. Hunting with a setter or a pointer is neither "game bag hunting" nor a fun day out. This is hunting in all of the purity of the art, in search of something more than mere efficiency. In addition to the satisfaction that these dogs give, there is also their special panache: these dogs are artists. When they succeed at something, it can often be considered a masterpiece. Like all artists, they are a little sensitive and like to be treated with empathy. However, if the hunter is brave enough to let these dogs express themselves with spirit and initiative, they can make the

Pointers, Setters, and Spaniels

Because it is sympathetic and a good performer, the English setter is currently the most frequently used pointing dog in the world.

pursuit sublime. Too many pointers and setters are victims of misunderstandings and excesses of authority. You must never confuse obedience, which is a product of training, with a short hunt. A short hunt is appropriate for certain breeds, regardless of their training, although at times it appears that the dog is not paying attention or is not following directions. To make these dogs track game under the gun is ridiculous. Great hunting goes hand-in-hand with independence, and you are never quite the

master of these dogs but rather a partner. If the terrain makes it necessary, they will shorten their search to stay in contact with the hunter. Again, there is no need to prefer a more placid breed. The main concern is to objectively choose the type of dog and the type of hunting that you want to pursue.

Experts at the wildest of game

The wide-open spaces and the wildest types of small game are certainly the preferred domain for these

breeds. You only need to watch a setter or a pointer working on small mountain game, such as woodcock under a stand of trees or snipe in marshland. Despite unfavorable and inaccurate prejudices, the British dogs have gradually conquered the hearts of many hunters. Some think it is a question of fashion, but do fashions ever last for very long? These long-range hunters enjoy immense popularity; on hunting grounds throughout the world, the English setter has become the breed most used by hunters of woodcock. Although a little less widespread, the pointer also occupies a very honorable position. These animals have descended from famous lines of Grand Champion, long-range hunters, and they offer a certain security. They are known for their athletic abilities, their noses, and their ability to freeze quietly. The upkeep of this breed benefits from a network of breeder contacts extending throughout Europe, which, added to their strong numbers, is very important. Unfortunately, today there are more good pointers around than hunting grounds to suit them.

THE BRITTANY SPANIEL: VERSATILITY AND EFFICIENCY

You can find other pointing dogs called Continentals everywhere in Europe, as with all of the brilliant British breeds. One of the most popular is the Brittany spaniel. The method by which it reached this level of popularity is particularly interesting. Initially, it benefited from the arrival of British dogs (mainly setters) on the Continent, at a time when most French breeds

found themselves being swept from the scene for the same reason. However, the Brittany spaniel possessed the extra qualities needed to make it flourish. Its history is the product of a chain of circumstances that favored the evolution

The Small Münsterlander is at home in open country, woodland, or marshes. They have a very fine sense of smell.

of the breed. Alliances, more or less deliberate to start with, produced lines of dogs that had fine noses, were firm in the point, were better built, and were overall more homogeneous. There is no doubt that the Brittany spaniel owes its extraordinary success to this breeding program. To some extent, it is what we would call a "crossbreed," the product of mongrels and purebreds that brought together the maximum qualities in the smallest volume. Paradoxically, the

The Brittany spaniel is a pointing dog of great merit.

Pointers, Setters, and Spaniels

Although less well known than those with orange-and-white coats, there are also black-and-white Brittany spaniels.

setters (to which it owes some of its abilities) find it a fierce rival that has successfully taken them on in competition. If the English setter remains the pointing dog most used by hunters of woodcock, the Brittany spaniel can be found relentlessly on its heels. It has avoided the pitfalls of specialization and has remained a very versatile dog, suited to hunting game birds and animals in forest, open country, or marshland.

Gentle and passionate

Generally speaking, the Brittany spaniel is an active dog that is early to mature. Its training should be without any problems, despite the fact that it sometimes behaves a little obstinately. In open country,

The German shorthaired pointer is largely unknown but is well-suited to hunting game, birds and animals.

The Picardy spaniel is one of the older breeds and is somewhat neglected by hunters.

it quarters the ground about 33-44 yards (about 30 to 40 m) ahead of its master, never neglecting possible hiding places for game. Because it does not run much, it discovers animals at a good distance, approaches, and stops. It makes this stop naturally, often in less time than other breeds, and then dashes easily after a bird taking flight. On a more practical level, it possesses formidable efficiency, particularly when in a concealed spot and on difficult terrain. Whether in a thicket, in an orchard, or under a large stand of trees, its small size allows it to turn sharply, making it a true expert with pheasant and woodcock. It is to this talent that it owes a large part of its success (if not its discovery as a hunter). It is also prized for hunting snipe and other wildfowl. Because it is robust and very little trouble, this breed is easy to handle during transportation by road and can hunt all weekend (and such stamina is valuable to a hunter with only one dog).

The Brittany spaniel is the ideal dog for the rough shooter who likes to tramp arround the countryside and flush out all kinds of game. It is a good domestic companion, as well as gentle, affectionate, and capable of those spontaneous bouts of affection so characteristic of spaniels.

Very versatile, the German pointer is the most popular of the Continental types.

Pointers, Setters, and Spaniels

With its one-color coat, the Weimaraner is one of the most appealing dogs within its group.

THE GERMAN POINTER: STEADY AND GOOD-HEARTED

Courageous and efficient, the shorthaired German pointer has gradually become the most widespread and the most popular of all pointers. It too belongs to the large family of Continentals. Its special features are a powerful physique, a short coat, a docked tail, and above all a characteristic versatility that is markedly superior to what is usually expected of a classic pointer. This must be because the regions from which it came had few hunting traditions, and therefore few hounds, leading hunters to use the same dogs for hunting both

French pointer.

small and big game. As well as possessing a talent for pointing game birds, it is an excellent tracker and is even good at getting onto the scent of wounded big game.

During the second half of the 19th century, the German pointer's breeding was directed toward creating a new type of dog, using animals which were less heavy and performed better than did the original type. It has never stopped evolving, yet has kept a remarkable homogeneity. However, it is true that only since the beginning of the 1960s did this breed conquer the hearts of large numbers of hunters, thanks to very good results in field trial tests. Today the German pointer is considered to be at the head of its group, with its numbers alone exceeding those of all other pointers combined. This is a dog of great merit.

A heritage which guarantees its possibilities

The German pointer is a dynamic partner, methodical, efficient, and consistent in its skills, whether in open

The Hungarian pointer is a powerful and enterprising dog that has quietly found a place in most European countries.

Quiet and talented, the Portuguese pointer is little known outside the Iberian Peninsula.

On the ground, the German pointer is a true performer, but it nevertheless requires a master who will exert a certain amount of authority. However, it has often been wrongly reported that the German pointer is a difficult dog. Rather, it is simply an animal of great character, which can be an asset to anyone looking for a partner capable of bringing in a big animal as well as a fire hare or a goose. Usually rather sizeable and a rustic yet well-rounded performer, the German pointer may appear to be a little aloof, but it is faithful and devoted.

country, woods, or marshland. Despite having a short coat and a fine hide, it never fears thorns, water, or bad weather. This breed has enough endurance for any test and is very determined in its movements. With a hunting style that is generally similar to that of its fellows, it rarely strays outside the range of the guns, quartering the ground in a regular pattern. Originally, the German pointer hunted with a fast, sweeping trot. Then, enthusiasts of the breed decided that they wanted a quicker dog, one that showed more enterprise and hunted at a gallop. When it catches the scent of game, the German pointer's movements become progressively more restrained. After a few strides at the trot, it will slow to a walk before stopping, with head up and ears raised. It is interesting to observe that the firmness of its pointing style does not at all detract from its other merits. Although it hunts nose-up, like an authentic pointing dog, it also puts its snout to the ground, making for a neat combination of scent-hunting and taking game directly.

A wirehaired variety of German pointer, the drahthaar is not without its charms.

Retrievers, Dogs for Flushing Game, and Water Dogs

The retrievers, dogs for flushing game, and water dogs are very specialized breeds that include in their numbers both those that are the rarest and those that are the most widespread.

The retrievers are used for hunting waterfowl and in battues for small game, where they fetch the fallen birds. What distinguishes them from other breeds is a great visual memory, known as the ability to "mark." The classification of the IHF lists six breeds, of which two come from North America (the Chesapeake Bay retriever and the Nova Scotia duck-

tolling retriever) and four come from Britain (the curly-coated retriever, the flat-coated retriever, the Labrador retriever, and the golden retriever). The great star of the group is definitely the Labrador.

A star dog, the Labrador can do just about anything.

THE LABRADOR – A LEGENDARY DOG

One beautiful legend says that Labradors might be the product of a match between an otter and a Newfoundland. While this breed is so common and widespread that it seems super-

fluous to give a chapter to it, it is still useful to recall the Labrador's hunting qualities. When a breed passes into posterity, it is usually not the result of rigorous breeding. The breed without doubt becomes an involuntary victim of good character and training skills. The

Mainly intended for driven game, the Labrador is an expert at retrieving wounded game.

With its flamboyant coat, the golden retriever enjoys enormous success.

dog of politicians, stars, blind people, and drug and explosives detectors, the Labrador remains very active at hunting events. It seeks wounded game, both big and small, and tracks waterfowl and game in open country and woodlands.

Although it seems that the Labrador can do everything, it is not a reason to let that occur. The Labrador is a lively and fast dog, but that does not mean it is unbeatable. The hunter must make it work or otherwise risk transforming it into a hound. The Labrador is born with many abilities, but it is not born trained. In order to favor these hunting lines, hunters organize specific field trials. Even though a Labrador might have the best will in the world, reliance on nature can never replace a true breeding program.

THE GAME-FLUSHERS: CHASERS FIT FOR ANY TEST

A kind of pointing dog that does not freeze, dogs for flushing game are determined and tenacious, and they glide about to "turf out" game using their own technique. They hunt by

Thanks to its hitting power, the spaniel is ideal for "turfing out" running birds.

combining the upper and lower scents of the game, which are the trail that the game leaves and the smells that lead to the shelter. They then briefly point and pursue the game, perhaps hoping secretly to grab it. Ideally, these dogs should remain still long enough for a shot to be fired, which in a blind (sometimes called a hide) can be very challenging, as there isn't much room for both the dog and the hunter. However, a dog that wants to charge also has the tendency to pursue. This is perhaps the only problem with training: teaching them to behave moderately when the bird takes off. Thus, they are to be recommended mainly for the hunter who has little experience in matters of training or who does not wish to spend much time on it.

The most widespread breeds are still the British spaniels, of which the cocker is the smallest and the most popular. Bred for its small size and a weight less than 25 pounds (about 10 kg), this breed soon carved out a reputation for hunting in the undergrowth. It quickly won success in the United States and Canada, but its status as a companion dog in those countries caused a number of disagreements with breeders who were quite determined to maintain its aptitude for hunting. Because it is easy to look after, the cocker does not need to be heavily groomed unless it is going to be shown, but a firm and regular brushing is still advisable. The cocker is a very active, passionate hunter with good endurance, and it has a strong personality expressed wonderfully in the most difficult terrain. It beats the territory in front of the hunter, at about mid-range for the guns, which makes it even more effective. It dives into thickets spontaneously and with determination; nothing can deter it, not even a bramble bush, the deepest ditch, or the marsh. Cockers prefer rabbits and running birds, such as pheasant. The woodcock is another type of game that offers the cocker some fine opportunities.

WATER DOGS

Water dogs make up a small family of very specialized breeds. Their specialization is sometimes seen as a detriment, because their highly refined talents appeal only to a small number of dedicated wildfowl hunters, who know that without such dogs a wounded bird is a loss. The exact origins of these dogs have become confused because they are very old. As with the retrievers, their use in maritime areas has always eased the way for exchanges between hunters from various coastal regions, such as England, France, Holland, and Portugal. The IHF has formed a specific category of water dogs, quite distinct from retrievers and game-flushers. Confined to a niche that is at the same time both narrow and saturated, the water dogs are victims of the constant reduction of marshland open to hunting and of competition from more versatile breeds. Thus the American water spaniel is still almost unknown, as are the Spanish water dog and the *lagotto romagnolo* (which comes from the lowlands of Comacchio and the marshlands of Ravenna, in Italy, where it has instead become a truffle hound in the plains and hills of Romagna as a result of the

The German Wachtelhund is an excellent flusher, determined and tenacious.

Retrievers, Dogs for Flushing Game, and Water Dogs

wetlands being drained). Thus, only four varieties now form the group: the water spaniel, the Portuguese water dog, the Irish water spaniel, and the wetterhoun, or Dutch water dog.

THE WATER SPANIEL: THE FOURTH MUSKETEER

The water spaniel is the only French breed of aquatic dog. It practices the oldest known forms of hunting, as it has been around for about 1500 years. With its vigorous appearance and squat form, it is characterized by a long, woolly mane that sometimes forms tufts. Its one-color coat ranges from black to white and through all shades of brown. It has a quick hunting style that is very methodical and conscientious, with inborn retrieving talent. Neither mud nor bad weather can stop it, because its fur can form a veritable carapace against the elements. Because of this, the water spaniel needs regular grooming if it is not to become, in the popular phrase, "filthy as a water spaniel."

The cocker is the smallest and the most common of all of the spaniels.

Greyhounds

Because they are highly valued in a large number of countries, hunting with greyhounds has helped to maintain some very old varieties.

Hunting with greyhounds is a highly prized activity on the entire Iberian Peninsula.

Greyhounds are unusual in that they make up a group of particularly homogeneous breeds. These original types, elegant and purebred, mostly have common origins on which their merits as hunters depend. On the other hand, unlike with all other varieties of hunting dog, their sense of smell has never been a determining factor in their breeding, since the various lines have been refined to improve the singular skill of simply outrunning. Thus, today's greyhounds resemble the oldest representatives of the entire heritage of hunting dogs.

The galgo is a true athlete.

THE SPANISH GALGO: LORD OF THE PLAINS

The tradition of hunting with greyhounds has always been very strong in England, Spain, and Portugal. Among hunters in the Iberian Peninsula, the term "galgo" means "greyhound" in a generalized way, whatever its breed or country of origin. This is

The saluki is distinguished by its half-long coat, but is not often seen at the hunt today, unlike in previous years.

because the Spanish galgo has been infused with greyhound blood to maintain its speed. This breed is probably one of the oldest greyhounds used exclusively for hunting. In addition to having a marathon runner's physique, it has a real flair for hunting. When it pursues game, always in pairs, it knows how to act in perfect harmony with its partner, how much effort to expend, how to anticipate the tricks and sudden swerves of the hare, and how to cut corners to intercept the game.

It is a redoubtable hunter that works by instinct, hunts by sight, and is never actually trained. It is a true virtuoso.

An authentic hunter

This formidable athlete, with a bigger heart than those of other hunting dogs, has an iron constitution and a very balanced, serious character, even to the point of sometimes being reserved. The greyhound's almond eyes, which give it a gentle and discreet look when at rest, light up like flares as soon as it spies the shadow of a game animal in flight. Quick as lightning, it dashes off at an energetic and very elastic gallop, which it will continue until it catches the animal. There are two varieties of galgo: one with a short, smooth, and very fine coat, and

another with a fairly long wirehaired coat that tends to form a sort of moustache. The latter is one of the rare greyhounds, because it has remained very popular yet never became the exclusive property of certain groups.

Now rarely found, the sloughi was a great specialist at gazelle hunting.

Today, hunting with greyhounds is limited to chasing hares and sometimes foxes.

EUROPEAN BIG GAME

Red Deer

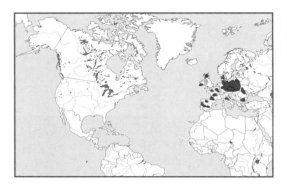

LATIN NAME:
Cervus elaphus

One of Europe's most imposing mammals, the red deer is distributed throughout Europe and Scandinavia.

DESCRIPTION

The red deer's size varies depending on the location and the individual. It can measure from 5 to 8 ft. (1.65 to 2.5 m) in length, with a height to the withers of 4 to 5 ft. (1.2 to 1.5 m) and an average weight of 270 lb. (100 kg) for the female hind and 400 lb. (150 kg) for the male stag. A few individuals close to 1070 lb. (400 kg) have been seen in the Carpathians. The antlers can weigh up

A subspecies found in Corsica and Sardinia: the Corsican deer (Cervus elaphus corsicanus).

to 40 lb. (15 kg). A tawny red or yellow coat protects the red deer. The chest is darkly colored in the male and gray in the female. A black line either runs along the back or occurs only on the neck. The calves wear a tawny coat marked with white until August, blending in perfectly with the background. The red deer molts first in May and then again in November.

HABITAT

Originally, the red deer lived in open country. It can still be found in Scotland in beautiful surroundings of smooth moorland, where it is perfectly acclimatized. The pressures of hunting and the development of agriculture have forced it into refuge in the forests. The red deer does not particularly like impenetrable massifs but instead prefers to colonize stands of trees. An agile animal, it is also perfectly at home in hilly terrain, and can be seen at altitudes up to 6560 ft. (2000 m) in the mountains. It swims readily and will not hesitate to cross rapids or large stretches of water when pursued.

The deer leaves its forest refuge to go to the feeding ground under cover of dusk.

Red Deer

Confrontation between two males during the rutting season.

DIET

The diet of the red deer consists of grass, buds, leaves, acorns, beechnuts, berries, and mushrooms, as well as potatoes, cereals, and fruits such as apples. In winter it subsists on dried grasses, heathers, and the bark of conifers or broadleaf trees. Each animal consumes about 40 lb. (15 kg) of food per day, with 30 percent of its diet consisting of woody or semi-

Velvet is a protective skin covering on new antlers.

woody vegetation, 10 percent fruits, and 60 percent herbaceous plants. It can damage crops such as corn on a large scale, as well as tree farms when it browses on the shrubs.

BEHAVIOR
The rut

The rutting period occurs between the middle of September and the middle of October. During this time, the forest resounds with the bellowing of the stags, a deep, powerful call. The stag uses this call to affirm his supremacy and provoke rivals. In this way, he draws his harem together, a herd consisting of about ten hinds that he protects jealously.

Gaston Phœbus described the rutting stag in his work dedicated to hunting:

"They are fierce at that time and will rush at men as would an excited wild boar. And they are dangerous beasts, for it is only with much difficulty that a man will recover if he is badly wounded by a stag. And for that reason people say: after the wild boar the doctor, after the stag the coffin. For it hits very hard, like the blow of a cudgel, such is the great strength it has in its head and body. They kill each other, wound and fight one another when they are in rut, that is to say in their love, and they sing in their own language as does a man in love. They kill dogs, horses and men in that time and bark like a wild boar, above all if they are tired; I saw one which wounded the groom, then chased and killed the bloodhound and, on top of that, a charger [horse]."

However, it appears that the fighting of stags takes up more space in stories than in real life. The fights between large, dominant males are always very violent, with the animals confronting each other, antler against antler. Sometimes the tines intertwine in such a way that these males become inextricably locked together and die from exhaustion. An unfortunate blow to the vital organs can bring

A deer with damaged antlers can inflict severe wounds on its fellows.

about the death of one of the stags. In most cases, however, one of the adversaries will abandon the fight when he feels overcome. The belligerence of the dominant male is also expressed at that time by curious behavior: at the height of its excitement, the stag will drive the tines of its antlers into the ground. These stags have also been observed getting angry at bushes, which they literally flatten.

After the rut, the males leave the female herds and take shelter within the deepest part of the forest. After winter arrives, they may rejoin the hinds, but during the entire summer season they tend to live alone or in small troops.

THE "MURDEROUS" STAGS

Although the antlers of the stag should never be viewed as mere weapons or as a means of prestige or seduction, it is important to remember that they are indeed formidable instruments, especially those belonging to the old stags that revert to savagery. They are highly dangerous during fights and can inflict mortal wounds, using their antlers as daggers: this is why they are sometimes called "murderous" or "killer" stags.

The hind usually gives birth to just one calf, which is protected by a spotted coat that blends in perfectly with its surroundings.

Reproduction

The hind gives birth to one calf on average between April and May, approximately 240 days after mating. The calf is suckled until the beginning of winter. For the first period of its life, the calf carefully hides in dense thickets, where the markings of its coat will blend in totally. The hind stays a good distance away from the calf but keeps a very careful watch. When night comes, the mother summons her young with a brief call to leave its shelter, and the little family leaves the wood, venturing closer to its edge or into a clearing.

Red deer are active not only at twilight but also shortly before sunrise. These two times represent their main peaks of activity. They rest during the day.

The herd

Red deer live in very structured, matriarchal communities: the hind, her calf, and the young from the previous pregnancy, which the mother abandons after giving birth again, form the basic family unit.

Several family units get together to form a herd, led by an old, experienced hind that ensures the cohesion and safety of the entire group.

The male deer older than three months resemble each other closely. From the stage of the "sixth tine," a young, dominant stag may appear in the group. When the rutting season arrives, it challenges one of the older stags to try to form its own harem.

Also worth mentioning are old "vagabond" stags, which do not occupy a particular territory and are timid and generally solitary. They may, however, have a younger companion, known as a "squire."

Young conifer tree farms may suffer badly from damage inflicted by deer, which are very fond of the buds and young shoots.

A herd of hinds and female juveniles is often led by an old, barren female.

SIGNS OF THE DEER'S PRESENCE

The red deer leaves many signs of its presence in any given territory. Certainly among the most visible are the hoofprints. They generally show only two cloven marks imprinted upon the ground, but can nevertheless reveal the pads if the animal has jumped. The average size of the print is 3 in. in length by 2 in. in width (7.5 cm by 5.5 cm). Another sign of the red deer is the wallow, a kind of muddy pond in which the deer, like a wild boar, likes to wallow before rubbing itself vigorously against the rough bark of a tree.

The droppings, deposited in small heaps, are about 1 in. (2.5 cm) long and have a long, cylindrical shape, slightly pointed at one end and flat at the other,

including a slight depression if the deer is male.

While resting in a shelter, the red deer leaves an impression of its body upon the ground, evidenced by crushed vegetation over a variable area.

Yet another sign is clear damage caused to plants, along with other marks of

feeding. Strip marks and signs of browsing at farms are evidence of recent feeding activities.

Friction marks on trees, about 6 ft. (2 m) above the ground, are caused by these deer removing damp earth which is clinging to their coats after bathing in wallows. When the deer sheds

Red deer hoofprints.

the velvet on its antlers, more signs of friction can be seen on shrubs.

RULES FOR GOOD MANAGEMENT OF DEER POPULATIONS

The primary objective of population management is to maintain a balanced number of deer that is compatible with the area's capacity to sustain them. This helps to prevent serious damage to crops and farms, and sustains a harmonious balance in the ratios of deer age to sex.

Another benefit of population management is to supply good culling animals, those great prize deer that have become too rare.

The best internal structure of a deer population is obtained by observing the following culling plan:
– 7 percent of old hinds and those with ten tines and over;
– 10 percent of adult hinds and those with fifth, sixth, seventh, eighth, and ninth tines;
– 20 percent of adult hinds not accompanied by young and those with second, third, and fourth tines;
– 20 percent of juveniles.

Never cull a lead hind, because an entire troop might break up completely. Keep the finely antlered males, as these half-grown animals are the guardians of the future of the species.

HUNTING DEER

Gaston Phœbus said, "They are light and strong animals and wonderfully wise. I declare it is the most noble form of hunting in which one can indulge." Thus the

It is advisable to cull the large, fertile males to ensure a good population balance.

Red Deer

deer is indebted to great people for having lasted longer than other animals in the civilized countries. Because the deer is the principal target of grand-scale hunting, the pleasures of the hunt have actually protected it.

Stalking

The main object of this type of hunting is to maintain a good balance in the deer population. Shooting should be done selectively in order to eliminate, first of all, small or sickly individuals. Because the red deer is normally a very discreet animal, the mating period seems to be the most favorable time to indulge in stalking, as the animals then lose some of their vigilance and are easier to approach.

Another good time to stalk is when the deer go to forage early in the morning or at dusk. The hunter must blend in perfectly with his surroundings and wear neutral-colored clothes. Some form of headgear should hide part of his face, and gloves should protect his hands. The hunter moves silently against the wind, prospecting clearings, forest rides, and edges of woods.

Every likely location should be carefully observed with the aid of powerful binoculars. The approach begins once an animal has been spotted, with the hunter

The animal is spotted in the binoculars. Should the hunter shoot?

Stalking requires that the ground be minutely examined beforehand.

This high seat has been judiciously located close to a feeding ground.

ready to freeze totally as soon as the deer shows any sign of anxiety. The shot is fired from a reasonable distance of around 110 yd. (100 m) toward the animal once it offers a well-outlined, side-on silhouette.

High seat shooting

The high seat shooting is another way of hunting that allows a carefully selected shot to be fired at deer when they are perfectly presented, calm and ignorant of the danger threatening them.

Of course, choosing a good place to locate the high seat, also called a deer stand, has a lot to do with ultimately being successful. It must be built near places regularly visited by the animals, such as feeding grounds with paths regularly marked by prints. It is often placed at a crossing of two rides, on the edge of the forest, or in a clearing.

There are several types of high seat. The simplest is a portable installation equipped with a seat on an extendable metal ladder, and the whole thing can be firmly secured to a tree trunk.

A large animal with superb trophy antlers.

Fixed installations can be much more sophisticated. They are almost like small houses about 30 ft. (10 m) off the ground, consisting of a roof, four walls made of logs, and firing windows. A small ladder provides access to the platform. The main advantage of a fixed installation is the comfort, as a good high seat can completely shelter the hunter from bad weather.

The hunter should discreetly settle into the high seat before dawn. If the ambush is to take place in the evening, the hunter will need to arrive at the high seat by mid-afternoon, well before the animals start moving toward their feeding grounds.

The path giving access to the installation must always be carefully maintained, with typical care taken to remove any twigs that might crackle underfoot and arouse the suspicions of deer resting nearby in the brush.

Silent Driving

This is a kind of battue that avoids the noise and "hue and cry" of the hunt. No packs of hounds here, at the very most the hunter may use one small, light-footed dog that merely flushes out the animals under the guns. The advantage of this method is clear: the deer

The end of a battue is handled briskly.

calmly and unknowingly offer themselves to the shooter in a usual hierarchical order, which helps the hunter avoid accidentally culling a lead hind. This is a way of carrying out a selective shoot in the best of circumstances, when the hunter is looking for first-year juveniles.

The "hue and cry" battue

This battue, practiced primarily in France and Spain, brings a large number of participants into the action. The battue begins at dawn, when efforts are made to locate the animals in a certain area by reading specific signs, such as fresh hoofprints and the remains of meals. The leader of the hunt, having reminded himself of the management rules to be applied in this territory, then declares how many animals may be culled that day according to sex and age ratios, and he also issues elementary instructions about safety to each of the shooters. Small dogs (such as a pack of fox terriers) or hounds (such as Anglo-French dogs) are then let loose upon the fresh scents.

The shoot is often carried out on moving targets, as hunters fire on fleeing silhouettes that leap over the forest rides with a single bound or standing jump. At the signal for the end of the battue, it is always necessary to verify that an animal has not been merely wounded. Drops of blood on the leaves or even a splinter of bone at the point of impact should compel the hunters to seek out the wounded animal, with the help of specific dogs.

The deer hunt

This deer hunt, also called a "venery," is a French form of hunting that has feudal origins and is still practiced by about 30 specialist groups, principally in the Massif Central and the great forested massifs of Sologne and Normandy. It begins at dawn with the "quest," undertaken by the bloodhound keeper, whose task is to control the dog. He covers the area to be hunted accompanied by an older, silent dog that merely pulls on its tether to signal the possible presence of an animal in a thicket. After reading certain signs – prints or cloven depressions, branches bent by the animal's head, hoofprints in moss or grass, or herbaceous plants flattened by the animal's weight – the keeper can precisely deduce the size, weight, and sex of the animal in hiding. A broken branch placed on the ground then marks the entry path of the deer. The keeper of the bloodhound gives detailed account to the leader of the hunt, who decides which animals to choose for the pursuit. Then the pack is let loose on the trail. If the keeper is not certain that a deer is hiding, then only a few very experienced, sharp-nosed dogs are set loose, called the "chasers." If he is certain, then the attack is made by the "death pack," with the entire pack, attack dogs as well as chasers, being sent in.

The deer will try many ruses to escape the dogs, never hesitating to cross pools and rivers, and take to stony paths where the trail becomes hard to follow. When these tricks fail and it is ringed in by the pack, the deer is finished off with a dagger or rifle shot.

The grand deer hunt is still a very prized form of hunting, particularly in France.

Roe Deer

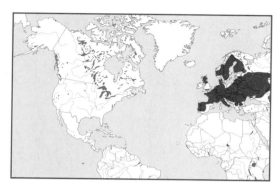

LATIN NAME:
Capreolus capreolus

Unlike many species that suffered from upheavals in the countryside at the end of the 20th century, the roe deer is gaining ground throughout Europe, especially in Germany, Britain, Switzerland, Austria, and France.

DESCRIPTION

The roe deer is the smallest member of the European *Cervidae* family. Its color (fawn or gray according to season), height to the withers of 25 to 30 in. (60 to 80 cm), and lack of a tail distinguish it from both the red deer and the fallow deer. The roe deer weighs between 55 and 65 lb. (20 and 25 kg). In winter, this animal has a pale gray coat with a white flash on the tail area. In summer, the coat molts and turns reddish-brown.

The male, called a buck, is distinguished from the female, or doe, by the

Roebuck surprised while feeding in a meadow at the forest fringes.

The characteristically graceful silhouette of a doe, which seems to have noticed the photographer's presence.

presence of antlers on its head. These are shed in November and grow back again at the end of winter. The two sexes can also be dis-

The velvet antlers are a sought-after trophy for hunters.

tinguished by the shape of the tail flash, heart-shaped in the female and bean-shaped in the male.

The antlers

From the age of six months, embryonic antlers appear in the male and are shed three months later. Then the growth of the true antlers begins under the protection of a downy skin called the "velvet." A buck usually has six tines (three on each side). The antlers grow larger over several years but then become smaller in old age. The antlers occasionally take on abnormal shapes. They may have "perruques," a kind of unsightly wart, or be misshapen. Some bucks are called "assassins" because they have antlers without tines, which are shaped like daggers and can be dangerous for other bucks. It is customary for hunters to eliminate these animals.

A SPECTACULAR DEVELOPMENT

This little deer owes its development to several factors: the institution of planned hunting, the conservation of the environment (the woods and forests), and the organization of a form of agriculture that it can make use of. One disadvantage is

Roe Deer

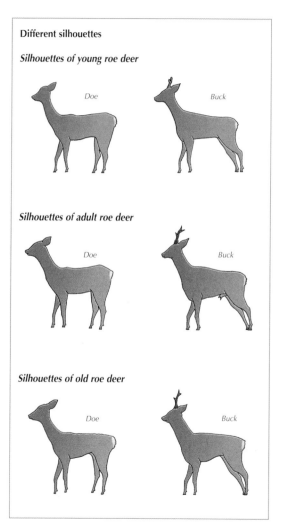

Different silhouettes

Silhouettes of young roe deer

Doe

Buck

Silhouettes of adult roe deer

Doe

Buck

Silhouettes of old roe deer

Doe

Buck

that serious epidemics, such as of liver fluke and strongyle nematode infection, can suddenly occur and periodically cause a significant number of deaths in the population.

HABITAT
The forest
The roe deer is primarily a forest animal that also

exploits dense thickets and the edges of the forest. A varied landscape that alternates between woodland, clearings, and cultivated areas suits it particularly well. The roe deer is very selective, feeding on bramble leaves, ivy, and other plants cut down in the felling areas, in clearings, or on the sunny fringes. Light

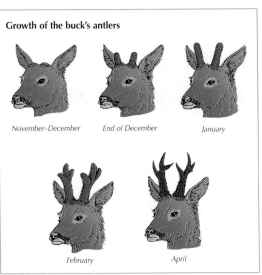

Growth of the buck's antlers

November–December

End of December

January

February

April

Bright and sunny clearings offer resting places that the roe deer appreciates.

and herbaceous layers and shoots are very important to this species. It leaves signs such as missing buds that have been browsed, stripped bark, and friction marks on young shoots where the male has rubbed its antlers.

In open country

With a strong ability to adapt, the roe deer has recently expanded its territory to the cereal plains, which it enlivens with its presence. Roe deer may live in groups on the plain. They lie down in the grasses and conceal themselves perfectly, arising only at sunrise and dusk.

Studies carried out in 1970 and 1981 over an area of 37,050 acres (15,000 hectares) in Poland revealed that roe deer have adapted wonderfully to this new way of life. It is rare to find these animals migrating. Bucks usually need about 370 a. (150 ha), while the does need about 345 a.

The daily diet of the roe deer varies according to the seasons. In summer, it especially likes grasses.

Doe and her kid feeding in a meadow.

(140 ha). The average life expectancy of the roe deer is fairly short: only 10 percent of the population studied lived for more than ten years. In these vast, cold areas the roe deer consume a lot of winter cereals, such as rye, oilseed rape, and alfalfa. They adapt more or less to the foods that are available.

The forest roe deer is a fairly solitary animal. In winter, the only period in which groups of roe deer can be observed, the social unit usually consists of a female, her two kids, and a male, probably a juvenile. However, roe deer gather in much larger units during the cold season in the open

country. Groups of more than ten animals were observed in the study area. This may be due to a defensive reflex on the part of animals because they feel more vulnerable to predators, but the relative crowding would seem likely to cause rivalries within the group. Confrontations are rare, however, for a simple reason: a hierarchy becomes established among the group members.

BEHAVIOR
Reproduction

Rutting takes place from the middle of May to the middle of June. The bucks confront each other, and some individuals may die

when their antlers become entangled. The buck is polygamous and tries to serve several does. During the rutting period, the bucks are particularly active, often "barking" and pursuing the females with this characteristic cry.

The kids are born ten months later. As a general rule, the doe raises two kids, but occasionally she may bear three.

A solitary homebody

The roe deer is a solitary animal that spends its life in just a few acres of woods. The bucks mark their territory and do not allow any rivals to enter, and they are individualistic and most often live alone, with little social activity. When winter comes, the animals regroup for a while before once again returning to their solitary ways.

AN ADAPTABLE ANIMAL

The roe deer has shown that it can adapt to very diverse surroundings. It lives equally well in woods, open country, marshland, or scrub. In France, it occupies almost the entire mainland area. According to the National Hunting Office, it uses all types of forest, such as stands of pine by the sea, beech groves, oak groves, and moorland with broom and gorse bushes. It has recently spread into the Mediterranean region and into mountainous areas.

A GAME ANIMAL SET FOR A FINE FUTURE

The roe deer is one of the rare European wild species with increasing numbers, to the great delight of hunters and naturalists. Its future is promising as long as it can continue to spread into many regions where its numbers are still low.

The large numbers of roe deer culled in Denmark (300,000 head) and Germany (1,023,082 head) show that the potential for development is considerable. The average number per cull is two head in France compared with forty-three in Denmark and six or seven in Germany.

The old bucks are cantankerous and can hardly bear their fellow deer.

Roe Deer

Roe deer can cause considerable damage to plantations.

Over-population is sometimes harmful

Even if this species does only scant damage to agricultural crops, its overabundance could bring problems for foresters. Those who depend essentially on forestry would be particularly vulnerable. The overabundant roe deer is not popular with foresters, because it eats buds on the trees and young plants. This is why specialist services plead for larger culls. In some areas, the hunters of hare think that there are already too many roe deer and that this deer disturbs their favorite game.

HUNTING ROE DEER
The battue

Each country has its own specialties. In England, Scotland, Austria, and Germany, they give priority to stalking, and the most classic form of hunting in France is the battue, with one line of hunters in fixed positions and another line walking forward.

Alert and disciplined beaters

Roe deer can be tracked in various ways: by entering the forest directly or by using a wider approach. The latter technique consists of pushing animals that exist in other areas toward the forest. The beaters must be disciplined, be able to keep pace with the advance, and look regularly to each side to ensure that everyone is walking in line. They are accompanied by hounds that give voice when the game is discovered. For this operation to succeed, it is better to place the beaters, whether they are armed or not, under the leadership of a keeper or an alert hunter who will use his little brass horn to communicate precise orders: advance, stop, begin the pursuit, and end the pursuit. The hunters in fixed positions must know this code, and they must not fire after the three blasts announcing the end of the

A pack of hounds under the whip of their keeper. The battue is about to begin!

pursuit. Unfortunately, this discipline is not always respected, but it does exist for everyone's safety.

A classic trick is to post one or two guns behind the beaters. Roe deer often set off in this direction. The guns shoot at the line of the forest track, without picking out particular animals. A hunt plan, made according to the density of animals in the region, gives a quota of heads to be culled. The cull must not amount to more than 20 percent of the animals available at the beginning of the hunt. A successful battue is one where everyone knows the safety rules, sticks to the target area, and does not try unlikely shots.

A convivial hunt

These battues have a notably atavistic character. Here you can find rituals, developed over the centuries, of the group as it shares the game. The division of game and the meal after the hunt are an extension of primitive hunts formerly indispensable to the survival of the group. As opposed to stalking, which is a solitary and elitist form,

A buck offers itself side-on, ideal for a stalker's shot.

Roe Deer

the battue remains a popular and convivial way of hunting.

Choice of weaponry
In a battue, it is undoubtedly best to use a single shot firearm. The Express rifle and the bolt-action rifle are the most suitable. The .243 Winchester is well suited for shooting the fairly light roe deer, but it is always better to stop the animal dead than to resort to seeking it out with bloodhounds. The structure of the bullet is very important, as it determines the expansion of the ogival head and thus the value of the hit and the resulting wounds. Shooting efficiency depends greatly upon this. Some ogival heads particularly well suited to roe deer are the KS from RWS, the ABC from Hirtenberger, and the Winchester Soft Point.

The silent "drive"
The silent "drive" variant is often practiced in Germany. The trackers advance quietly to avoid disturbing the game. There are no dogs, and the goal is to get the animals to cross the line of fire at a walking pace so that they can be identified (which is not possible in classic battues where animals are often going too fast to clearly distinguish them from one another).

Stalking
Stalking is indisputably the most effective way to hunt roe deer. It is a very prized method in Great Britain, Germany, and France. Stalking is considered an intelligent way to hunt because the shooter actually chooses his animal. It takes place in summer at dawn or at dusk when the animal is up and on its way to feed. The stalker moves forward like a shadow in the wood. He is dressed to blend in with his surroundings, and he keeps a careful eye out

A shooting position like this gives a perfect view of the course of a battue.

not to crack twigs underfoot. With a little practice, the hunter can get very close to any animal, roe deer as well as wild boar, rabbits, and hares.

Equipment

Equipment consists of a pair of high-powered binoculars with excellent lenses (with an enlargement power between seven and ten), indispensable during the hours of twilight, and a rifle with a scope sight that has variable magnification and a large object lens.

A rigorous cull

The stalker works with surgical precision. The rule is to cull one-third juveniles, one-third bucks, and one-third does older than one year. The stalker shoots small or sick animals, those that are late molting, those

Stalking enables a careful, selective shot to be fired, thus eliminating substandard or surplus animals.

with spindly or misshapen antlers, bucks with humps, and old animals in decline. Shooting a few fine bucks with antlers at their peak is a reward for good management. The stalker can take excellent trophies from bucks between four and ten years old. From its fourth year, a buck will probably have bulky and heavy antlers, and the best animals always mature early.

Shooting

The shot must be decisive, so it is best to hunt with a break action gun or a bolt-action rifle. Some people favor a set trigger (which makes it much more sensitive), others prefer to have firm control. It is merely a matter of individual taste. Using a firing rest is a very practical way to hold the rifle and avoid any vibrations. You can

A difficult but passionate hunt has been crowned with success.

Roe Deer

create a firing rest by cutting a branch that has a small fork, or you can buy an actual tripod at a gun shop. Shoot as near as possible – less than 110 yd. (100 m) – and take care to adjust for an animal moving across the line by aiming above the front hoof.

Classical hunting (venery)
Classical hunting for roe deer is a Franco-Belgian specialty. It consists of hunting the animal down and letting the dogs kill it.

The hunts
Venery is a traditional way of hunting practiced for centuries, the rules of which were established in the 17th century. Mostly consisting of societies, the teams are placed under the technical direction of one or several hunt masters. Dress has a traditional and practical appearance, and each team is free to choose its own colors. Teams have unique buttons on their uniforms, considered the true distinctive sign of each team.

The Venery Society
Members of teams and their followers are grouped together in the Venery Society, an association founded in 1907 according to the law of 1901. About 300 pursuit-hunting teams have their own private association, the French Association of Venery Teams.

The pack
Hunting roe deer by venery is a refined form of hunting that cannot be learned in just a few seasons. The scent of the roe deer is very light, and the animal is full of tricks. A good team strikes about once every three outings. It is customary to use a pack of 30 to 40 dogs. These are large, swift, robust gun dogs. The Gascon blue and the French Poitou varieties are the most prized.

The hunting plan
In France, the holder of the right to hunt puts in a request to the Federation, which sends him a form. He must then supply details of his territory, the density of the roe deer population, and his culling preferences. The Federation sends the file to the Departmental Directorate of Agriculture, which calls together the commission for hunting plans. This is chaired by the prefect or his representative, and brings together repre-

Hunting roe deer by venery is the most difficult method.

FRANCO-ISRAELI ROE DEER

The acclimatization of roe deer moved from the forests of Chizé in France to the Israeli reserve of Mount Carmel is continuing in difficult conditions. Israel stands at the eastern limit for the natural distribution of roe deer, and after this animal disappeared from the region for 70 years, the local authorities decided to reintroduce it. The reintroduction program for the roe deer is part of a developmental policy for natural surroundings and wildlife. There is now a string of reserves that runs from the north to the south of Israel. There you can find ibex, addax, ostrich, the very rare Mesopotamian

fallow deer, and oryx. These roe deer must cope with difficult conditions. Of four animals released, three have died, killed by jackals and wild boar, which are enormous in this region. One has disappeared, perhaps to poachers. Taking births into account, only 16 are left.

sentatives of the hunters and of the agricultural and forestry communities. It decides upon the numbers to be culled, taking into account the management requirement. If they wish, they may decide to either maintain a population or to increase or reduce it. The culls may thus vary from one-fifth of the number present the previous spring to one-third, if a population should be reduced because it is causing too much damage. The holders of hunting plans can appreciate that they are part of a collective decision.

The opinions of keepers and technical people, who know the question well, are an additional safeguard. Of course, even then mistakes can be made and some may feel wronged. In general, however, this system has proven itself to be quite effective.

Wild Boar

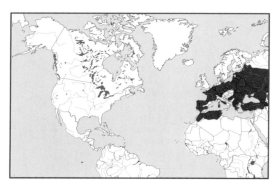

LATIN NAME:
Sus scrofa

This large male digging in the mud has just spotted the photographer.

Following the example of the roe deer, the wild boar has developed at a spectacular rate throughout Europe, to such a point that the damage it causes has caused true problems for farmers.

DESCRIPTION

The wild boar belongs to the large *Suidae* family, which includes all of the pig-like animals. Found on every continent, the wild boar can breed with a domesticated pig, which explains the sightings of boar colored pink and white or black and white. Corsica, for example, no longer has any pure wild boar strains.

The wild boar's snout is flattened like that of a pig,

enabling it to eat like its domestic cousin by digging around in the ground. It is capable of turning over a field of potatoes within just a few hours.

The wild boar's tusks are two pair of elongated, sharp, white teeth (one upper pair and one lower) that have grown outward.

Wild boar are omnivorous and especially like this kind of meadow, rich in plants and other species.

It is well protected by this coat, which shelters it from bad weather. This animal likes to wallow in mud, which forms a crust when it dries and prevents parasites – most notably ticks – from attacking it.

Its hooves consist of a cloven forefoot with two spurs behind it. Thus, the prints can be easily identified, since the red deer and roe deer that live in the same forests do not have rear spurs on their hooves.

HABITAT

The wild boar lives chiefly in large and sometimes small forests, but it may also settle in the scrub and even in cornfields.

Wild boar are gregarious and live in herds. They are wanderers, ceaselessly on the move, and they are essentially active at night. However, this animal's domain is not very big, ranging from 495 to

The head of the wild boar, bristly and armed with tusks.

The tusks growing from the lower jaw are tapered and cut like razors and are extremely dangerous. Those in the upper jaw are considered the upper canines.

The wild boar's coat is rough and gray or black.

DAMAGE PREVENTION

Wild boar cause terrible damage in fields. While repellants and acoustic devices never do much good, electric fences are efficient, or grain treatment can dissuade them. The Germans put grain in bottles, which serves to keep the offending animal in one place as it spends a lot of time trying to extract the grain. Using a barrel with holes is also effective. The barrel is attached to a chain that is fixed to a tree. Another method is to dig furrows and throw grain into them before covering it over. The aim is always the same: to keep the animal in one spot for as long as possible.

Wild Boar

Wild boar like this kind of boggy ground.

12,350 a. (200 to 5000 ha) according to the season.

It is possible to maintain a population on about 74,100 a. (30,000 ha), even in places where pressure from hunting is low or non-existent. In general, the wild boar's resting period lasts for half of the daily cycle, time spent seeking out food takes up a quarter of the day, and time spent moving about takes up the remaining quarter. As a wanderer, the wild boar is happy to expand its habitat if it cannot find any more food. A young male may thus have a series of shelters up to 4 mi. (6 km) from each other. On average, a boar

The wallow is a pool in which the wild boar rolls about, before rubbing against a tree with rough bark.

travels from 1 to 10 mi. (2 to 15 km) a day and explores an area of 10 to 75 a. (5 to 30 ha).

DIET

The wild boar lives chiefly in woodland. It is an omnivorous animal, which means it eats everything: grain, various grasses, roots, vegetables, carrion, eggs, and even small animals. The quality of its diet has important physiological consequences. A large crop of acorns in the forest can cause a female to mature early, with the average size of the resulting litter increasing along with the number of wild sows in gestation.

BEHAVIOR
Reproduction

The rut takes place between November and January. After a little more than three months of gestation, the sow bears three to six young. At the age of six months, the young lose their striped coats and become fine-looking "red beasts." The sows, with

Typical behavior by a large male in the rutting period: this one is marking trees to alert possible rivals to its presence.

Wild Boar

People say that the young, striped boars are "in livery."

These very young, suckling boars are still dependent upon their mother.

their young still in their first year, group together in twos and threes to form a small herd. At about the age of one, the males leave their mothers and form groups of young adults that gravitate around the herds. A young animal can be easily distinguished from a "red beast." With age, however, it becomes more difficult to tell either their age or their sex.

SIGNS OF THE WILD BOAR'S PRESENCE

These animals feed mainly at dawn, at dusk, or during the night, and they are rarely ever seen in the daytime. It becomes necessary to look at the ground to discover if a wild boar has left any revealing signs.

Prints

The prints of the wild boar, measuring from 2 to 3 in. (5 to 8 cm) long, are formed by the cloven forefoot and the pads, as well as by a rudimentary hoof shaped deeper at the back the heavier the animal is. The pads are somewhat closer together in the female and more broadly spaced out in the male. An old wild boar leaves very spaced-out marks, with the cloven part long and rounded from much use.

The tracks

The distance between steps is from 2 to 4 in. (5 to 10 cm) in the young, 4 to 6 in. (10 to 15 cm) in the females, and 4 to 8 in. (10 to 20 cm) in the males. Sows have cloven hoofs turned slightly inward, with those of the males turning outward.

Rooting and digging signs

The wild boar turns over the soil while looking for acorns, beechnuts, potatoes, and roots. It does this equally in the plains, in meadows, and on cultivated land. When looking for beetle grubs and other insects near the surface of the ground, it digs shallow furrows, called the "root marks." If it senses roots lying more deeply buried, it makes larger excavations from 10 to 20 in. (30 to 50 cm) deep, called the "dig marks."

The droppings
The droppings are about 4 in. (10 cm) long and take the shape of small, dark rolls that are loosely heaped together.

The resting place
The resting place is the wild boar's refuge, a simple depression hollowed out beneath a bramble, always dry and sheltered from the wind. This animal makes its resting place in the densest part of the wood, in impenetrable massifs where it can remain undisturbed.

The wallow
The wallow, a small pool in which the wild boar refreshes itself, should not be confused with the resting place. These animals love to roll in the mud and then rub against the trees to rid themselves of ticks.

A wild boar in its summer coat, which is short and fairly thin.

IS IT SEDENTARY OR MIGRATORY?
For a long time, people have thought that wild boar were migratory animals that could travel considerable distances. Scientific research has shown this to be a false assumption.

Wild boar are much more sedentary than was though at the beginning of the 19th century, even if a few do manage great journeys.

For a group of stable and sexually active animals in some regions, the annual territory will not extend beyond 12,350 a. (5000 ha). This finding is the result of studies carried out in the Mediterranean region of southern France on animals that had been tagged with transmitters. More than half of the marked animals remained faithful to the area where they were born, since they were killed less than 3 mi. (5 km) from where they were tagged. Within a larger circle 5 mi. (10 km) in diameter, 73.1 percent of the animals were traced. Thus, nearly three-quarters of wild boar are considered to be static. Larger movements in excess of 25 mi. (40 km) were traced to only 4.3 percent of the total number.

These nomads were farm-bred animals released to increase the regional population. The record, held by an animal killed in a hunt, is about 90 mi. (140 km) from the place where it was tagged. This is an exceptional example.

THE BENEFITS OF MANAGEMENT
Good news has come from eastern Europe via

A herd, including one animal on the right that is definitely the lead sow.

The battue is a convivial event that is much enjoyed throughout southern Europe.

how resistant the animal is to bullets, especially if they are badly placed. In killing it, the hunter is aware both of doing something good – the damage that the wild boar causes is considerable – and of having fired a superb rifle shot. When a herd of wild boar is discovered, a battue is rapidly organized.

Germany. The people responsible have started managing wild boar just as they do roe deer and red deer.

This Germanic system has progressively worked its way into France with selective shooting of juveniles (priority given to the young and the "red beasts"), respect for the lead sow, the installation of special game reserves to protect the fields, shooting with rifles, and "silent drives" which allow time to identify animals crossing the line of fire. Hunters have recognized by now that, by laying down rules, they could have a larger and healthier population.

The wild boar fires the imagination of hunters in Italy and the south of France. However, the maquis landscape in these areas is not very suited to selective shooting: just take a look at a wild boar galloping through the undergrowth!

HUNTING WILD BOAR

Hunters nurture a passionate feeling for the wild boar. They respect its strength and brutality and know

A resourceful and cunning animal

Either in a battue or during a stalk, wild boar hunts are never automatically crowned with success. This animal is remarkably intelligent and has no equal at detecting the whereabouts of hunters and avoiding them. In some daylight hunts, wild boar know the

---

GOOD CALIBERS

Hunting wild boar with a rifle using cartridge of lesser power than the 7 mm Remington is not a good idea. However, using a weapon of more than 9 mm is excessive. A good choice is somewhere between the two, within a range of about 30 calibers. The .300 Winchester Magnum, the 7 x 64, and the 8 x 57 JRS are considered classics. The good old Brenneke slug, used in smoothbore guns, gives a good result as long as the hunter fires at short range. The Brenneke slug has good precision up to about 65 yd. (60 m) – beyond that, this ammunition is risky.

Wild boar, discovered thanks to an excellent bloodhound, the Hanover red.

shooting positions so well that they can judge to within virtually a meter where to safely leave the forest. If the shooting positions are too close together, they will refuse to leave their patches. The old, solitary boar in particular listens with all of its senses strained to determine the source of danger. Instead of fleeing at top speed, it slips silently away. These big boars seem to transform themselves into field mice to escape their pursuers, as no one ever sees them leave their positions. You can sometimes even find them approaching the hunters noiselessly, waiting until other terrified animals have taken the bullets, and then with one bound they cross the firing line to safety when the weapons are no longer loaded.

A much coveted game animal

Shooting a wild boar, even if it is not an old, solitary animal, remains engraved forever in the heart of the hunter, especially when it is his first. When a young man kills his first wild boar in Spain, his fellow hunters hold a special ceremony for him. The more experienced hunters pour a mixture of the boar's blood and entrails over the hunter's head. This may seem a repugnant ritual, but its aim seems to be to bind hunters and game together for life, not unlike the "blood pacts" of some Native American tribes.

Small hounds can get into thick bramble bushes more easily.

Wild Boar

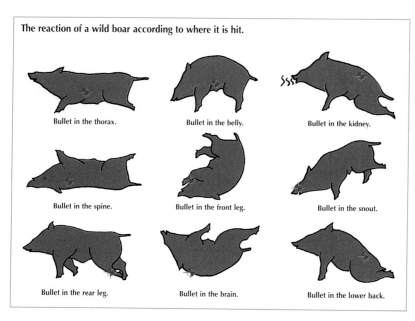

The reaction of a wild boar according to where it is hit.

Bullet in the thorax.

Bullet in the belly.

Bullet in the kidney.

Bullet in the spine.

Bullet in the front leg.

Bullet in the snout.

Bullet in the rear leg.

Bullet in the brain.

Bullet in the lower back.

Hunting with hounds

When the hunt is a battue, the use of a specially trained bloodhound can turn out to be valuable for discovering the hollows where the animals made their resting places. Then the guns can be positioned before the area is raided with the dogs. Most dog breeds love hunting wild boar.

A good beater

A good beater must never get out of line without the express order of the hunt master. He must not hesitate to beat bramble bushes,

and he must learn the different calls and instructions of the head tracker, while watching the dogs and observe how they bark and yelp. If he has little chance of shooting, he must be ready to "see off" a wounded boar that could be a danger for the dogs if still on its feet.

The wild boar will not hesitate to turn around and jump into the only dead ground in the plan of attack. For this reason, at least one gun should be placed in the back, behind the beaters.

First identify, then fire at a vital spot

This animal is remarkably resistant. Boar have been hit ba large bullets and kept running as if nothing happened. It is not the caliber that assures the kill but rather the placing of the bullet, which must without question hit the animal's front end. A bullet in the neck or the temple is a fatal blow, whereas one in a lung or the belly is a bad hit. As most fatal accidents happen in the course of these hunts, the hunter must neither fire while tracking nor fire at any animal that has not been properly identified. A bullet can sometimes only wound a wild boar, but it will likely kill a man every time. This is why many hunt organizers break out in a cold sweat when they organize battues that involve small-game hunters who lack experience.

Waiting in position can take a long time, but this is not the time to start moving about. Experience proves that the animal will jump into action when least expected.

Which animal to shoot?

Above all, do not shoot the lead sow, because her young, deprived of a mother, will die. It is normal to shoot either animals of less than 135 lb. (50 kg) or the youngest of these, which will help the herd to prosper.

Watch out for wounded boar

Fatal blows occur in only four areas: the spinal column, the heart and lungs, the head, and the abdomen. All others generally only cause wounds that are more or less serious. In addition, no hits actually bring about instant death. A fallen boar is not necessarily a dead boar. A boar that sustains a hit may not even notice its wound. The trace of the bullet must be looked for on the ground. If it is not found or if there is any doubt, then

Nose to the ground, a Hanover red follows the trail of a wounded wild boar.

a hunt must be started to find the wounded animal. Cutting a branch or placing a white handkerchief at head height can mark the trail of the wounded boar's prints. Using a good bloodhound will perhaps help find the animal. A wounded wild boar is a dangerous

Setting off on a difficult search for an animal that has left few signs of its wound.

A watchtower built close to a clearing where wild boar come to feed.

animal that will, without hesitation, charge a dog or a man who has unwisely come too close. If the animal has been discovered, it must be approached from the rear and then shot through the head.

Hunting from a high seat

Hunting from a high seat is also a prized method of hunting wild boar. The hunter must take up position in a fixed or mobile structure located on the fringes of the forest, getting inside before the animals come out of the trees at dawn or dusk. Hunting from a high seat is selective because the hunter has plenty of time to observe

PRACTICE ON A RUNNING BOAR

To adjust a rifle or learn to fire better in a battue, there is nothing like firing at a dummy boar. However, firing ranges equipped with these are not very common. This device consists of a target, representing a wild boar, that travels on rails at a variable distance from the shooter. The hunter can adjust his rifle perfectly under the guidance of experienced instructors at the firing range.

the animals closely through binoculars before firing. It is also very effective when the hunter has discovered where the animal usually goes to feed.

Taming a wild boar

This is a classic adventure: after a hunt by battue, you see the young boar rush out onto the forest trails. Some follow their mother, and others risk being gobbled up by the dogs. Many tender-hearted hunters think of adopting the orphans. A small wild boar is an admirable subject for adoption, as it is actually one of the few game animals that becomes friendlier in captivity. However, before giving in to this impulse, the hunter should remember that inside every domestic animal slumbers a wild one. An adult wild boar, even if friendly, is nothing like a young one. There have been a number of instances of dramatic accidents involving hunters who adopted wild boar.

Feeding and care

The young boar can be raised on bread dipped in milk. As soon as it becomes a "red beast," it lives up perfectly to its status as an omnivore and eats just about anything, from potatoes to the carcass of a chicken, small cakes, ears of corn, meat, eggs (rotten or otherwise), and lettuce. It's important to note that a wild boar gives off a strong smell of licorice, agreeable to some but unbearable to others, and that in a few months it will transform its enclosure into a battlefield.

A herd crosses a ride in hierarchical order; at the front of the group is the lead sow.

Corsican Moufflon

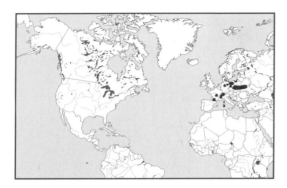

LATIN NAME:
Ovis musimon

Prince Bonaparte thought it was an antelope, and the naturalist Buffon called it a "wild sheep." This typical inhabitant of the mountains of Corsica and Sardinia came into being in Neolithic times, when hardy sheep brought in by sea reverted to a wild state.

A GREAT ABILITY TO ADAPT

The moufflon became a game animal at the beginning of the 19th century in central Europe, then western Europe and beyond (United States, Russia, Hawaii, and the Kerguelen Islands in the Indian Ocean), and the stock has been hybridized many times with sheep and other moufflon.

The worldwide population of moufflon has been estimated at 25,000 head, with 4500 in continental France. In Corsica, the present population amounts to between 400 and 600 head divided between two principal groups, on the slopes of Monte Cinto and on the peaks of Bavella.

DESCRIPTION

The true Corsican moufflon, which has not been hybridized, is also the

A rather unusual image: a lamb seen alongside several mature males.

Although the Corsican moufflon has a reputation for being a robust mountain animal, it actually avoids snow that has packed too thickly.

smallest, with a shoulder height of 25 to 30 in. (65 to 75 cm) and a weight of 70 to 95 lb. (25 to 35 kg) for females and 95 to 150 lb. (35 to 55 kg) for males. The males have strong, curved horns that can measure up to 35 in. (90 cm).

The appearance of the horns is very useful for judging the age of the moufflon. In addition, moufflon ewes may sometimes have horns. While they are abnormal among Sardinian females, more than half of Corsican females have them. These are thin, with parallel edges and a slight inward curve. The moufflon's coat is not wooly and is pale brown in summer, and then it darkens between the autumn molt and spring. Permanent white patches at the extremities of the limbs, the muzzle, and the hind-quarters make these animals

Young male about two-and-a-half years old: age can be judged on the basis of how curved the horns are.

easier to spot. The facial area of the females, called the "facial mask," varies in proportion with age. The "saddle" is a whitish patch that may appear on the flanks of males over two years old.

HABITAT

The moufflon's typical habitat is the mountains of the Mediterranean. However, occupation of any particular type of habitat is closely bound to the seasons. In winter, snow drives the moufflon down to the lowest altitudes of their range, onto the open slopes, and into the forest and the maquis scrubland.

Large male displaying the characteristically comical expression it generally wears before mating.

The rocky domes, which accumulate and retain what little solar warmth there is in winter, are often frequented at this time. The dense forests and the maquis also provide an effective shelter against the icy wind, as well as providing a large part of the moufflon diet. Its Mediterranean origins make the moufflon rather sensitive to the cold, and it pays a heavy tribute in hard winters. When spring returns, the moufflon again find the right amount of food, based on young shoots and herbaceous plants. Then, in scattered herds, they return to the slopes as the snow disappears. After five months of gestation, the females are ready to give birth and often separate themselves, along with their offspring born the previous year, from the rest of the herd. They give birth to a single lamb each year.

The moufflon settle into their summer quarters near the peaks, sheltered from insects and the fierce heat in mountain alder groves. They leave these refuges at dusk or dawn to feed. At that time of year in Corsica, they stuff themselves with "moufflon grass."

The finest population of moufflon today, which amounts to several hundred animals, exists in the massif of Caroux-Espinouse in France. The lowest foothills of the Massif Central, which dominate the Mediterranean, are strangely like a Corsican landscape. It is a wonderful opportunity for hunters who enjoy stalking.

BEHAVIOR
Reproduction

The arrival of autumn marks the mating season. Both sexes achieve sexual maturity at one-and-a-half years old, but sexual fulfilment in the male depends upon the hierarchy created by its age and the size of its horns. The males are very mobile at this time, and their mobility both encourages conflicts between them and fosters a continual mixing of the herds. The jousts that they participate in have no purpose other than to assure a momentary dominance in the herd of the winner and to establish a prerogative before mating with receptive females in rut.

These fights are spectacular but rarely fatal. In most cases, they boil down to formal symbolic acts (earning respect, avoidance, allegiance, and appeasement) by poses and contacts stripped of all violence.

Age groups	Percent culled	Criteria for killing
Lambs	30 percent	Must weigh 40 lb. (15 kg) at three months. Puny specimens are first priority.
One year	20 percent	Judge the quality of the juvenile's coat and bodily development. Hybrids are killed.
Adults	10 to 15 percent	Size and shape of the trophy are essential.
Old animal	30 to 35 percent	Abnormal shapes require elimination.

THE RULES FOR RECOMMENDED CULLS

Every self-respecting hunter covets the largest moufflon trophies. To obtain a harmonious population development and a perfect balance in terms of age and sex, it is a good idea to follow a rigorous culling plan, the details of which are given below.

HUNTING MOUFFLON
A difficult stalk

The moufflon is a very suspicious animal and is one of the most difficult to get close to. This assertion is somewhat contradicted by what certain old Corsican shepherds (poachers) have to say: "You know you have been spotted as soon as you hear this strident hiss they make when they are afraid. But this cry of alarm does not

always mean it is definitely going. Moufflon, especially the males, often turn back to have a look at the intruder." This curiosity must often have proven fatal when the moufflon was faced with a loaded gun. This animal's propensity to take flight

depends as much on its sex and age as it does on the surrounding plant cover, the lay of the land, the climate, and the season.

Beyond 210 yd. (200 m), the furthest range for shooting, the moufflon is sometimes just content to watch an

A three-year-old male moufflon stalked in the Massif Central mountains in France, where the species has been successfully introduced.

Three-year-old male, shot after a stalk in the Puy de Sancy, France.

cry of alarm, the coveted animals disappear.

To avoid this kind of trouble, which is always a bad experience after several hours of approach work in difficult terrain, the only solution is to attack the moufflon from the top of the mountain. This quarry animal is forever on guard and is always suspicious of danger coming from the valley, but rarely when it comes from above.

Firing

The shot should be fired at a reasonable distance – 90 to 110 yd. (80 to 100 m) – toward animals that have been clearly identified and that offer themselves in the best position.

High velocity, flat shooting cartridges are recommended, such as .270 Winchester, a 6.5 x 68, and possibly 7.64 in the range of light and fast projectiles. Keep in mind the size of the animal.

In cases when the hunter has apparently failed, it is essential to establish whether any kind of wound – fatal or otherwise – has been sustained by the moufflon.

intruder out of the corner of its eye while quietly carrying on its feeding activities.

A ewe on the lookout

In most cases, the indiscreet hunter will be quickly discovered by the lead ewe, which is always on guard and keeps herself carefully out of the way.

The hunter assumes that the approach has been successful. The animals seem calm and confident, and the herd is gathered on a grassy berm, completely oblivious of their surroundings. However, some distance away on a rocky promontory, the inconspicuous sentry is on the lookout. After a brief

Chamois

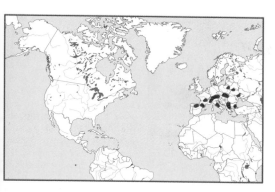

LATIN NAME:
Rupicapra rupicapra

The antelope of the peaks and the lord of the mountains, the chamois haunts the tallest and most majestic summits.

DESCRIPTION

The appearance of the chamois varies considerably according to its geographical location. Considered a separate species, the izard or Pyrenean chamois (*Rupicapra pyrenaica* – Bonaparte, 1845) is smaller and redder in summer. The chamois of the Cantabrian Mountains is smaller and paler than the izard. Also worth mentioning is the Apennine chamois of the Abruzzi region (*Rupicapra pyrenaica ornata* – Newmann, 1899), which is clearly distinguished from its cousins by the presence of two black lines on each side of the neck that frame the white of the throat and run down to the top of the breast.

The Balkan chamois differs from the others in several aspects of its head and horns, which are long, very curved, and spreading.

The Chartreuse chamois (*Rupicapra rupicapra cartusiana* – Couturier, 1938) is squat with short legs, and

In winter, the chamois is protected by a thick coat in shades between charcoal gray and black.

Chamois

Determining sex from chamois horns

Female's horn.

Male's horn.

it is on average heavier than the Alpine chamois. A small, very isolated population can be found in the Chartreuse Massif of France. Finally, there is the Carpathian chamois, which is the largest of all chamois. The male sometimes weighs more than 160 lb. (60 kg) and has a completely black coat in winter.

The chamois' designation as "antelope of the peaks" certainly comes from an extraordinary ability to adapt, developed in order to survive at high altitudes. Its hooves have a flat, rubbery sole that provides an excellent grip on slippery rock. Its heart weighs about 11 oz. (350 g), compared to 8 oz. (250 g) for that of a man. In addition, the chamois has red corpuscles estimated at 12 million, compared to 5 million for a man. These physiological and morphological adaptations give the chamois a rare capacity to withstand the difficult conditions imposed by the high mountains.

Male and female chamois have horns that develop permanently from the age of three to four months. Study of these horns makes it possible to judge the age and sex of the animal. For example, the hooks at the ends of the horns are more noticeably closed in the male than in the female.

HABITAT

Chamois live at different levels according to the season. In winter, they descend into the forested massifs at medium altitude, about 3300 ft. (1000 m). In summer, they venture further up onto the glaciers at around 9900 ft. (3000 m), though they only linger a short time due to the scarcity of food. Throughout the autumn, they wander about in large groups in the alpine pastures until shortly before the rut.

Otherwise, the chamois live in small groups consisting of females accompanied by their kids and juveniles from previous pregnancies, led by an old ewe. The bucks live somewhat isolated lives, however, without totally deserting the herd or the company of other males.

The Pyrenean chamois, or izard, is not as big as its alpine counterpart.

An izard and her kid, stationed on a rocky spur.

DIET

It is difficult to be completely certain about the daily diet of the chamois, which depends on the seasons and the availability of food.

According to the French naturalist Couturier, the basis of the chamois diet is alpine clover, plus plantains and various grasses. In winter, it consists of pine needles, ground ivy, and even rhododendron leaves. They also love salt and will seek out rocks with natural deposits.

BEHAVIOR
Reproduction

The rutting period extends from November to the beginning of December. During this time, fights and chases can be observed among the males, who seek to assert their dominance over a flock.

Neither blizzards nor deep snow seem to inconvenience the chamois.

After 170 days of gestation, the ewe gives birth between April and May to a single young or occasionally to twins. The kid is suckled for two to three months.

Active mainly during the day

The chamois is one of the few game mammals that has adopted an almost exclusively daytime existence, with the two peaks of activity given over to searching for food at dawn and at dusk. During the course of the day, they rest in the shadow of a rock or shrub, calmly ruminating.

An animal destined for a rugged life

Apart from man, the chamois has few enemies. Among natural predators are the wolf, the lynx, and the golden eagle, which attacks the weak kids. The highest mortality rate (up to 50 percent) is among the infant to one-year-old group. In addition to being constantly preyed upon, the chamois must also

Chamois

cope with the ruggedness of the climatic conditions in winter. The chamois is also the victim of a number of diseases caused by viruses and parasites. Purulent conjunctivitis can blind it, and strongyle nematode infection, papillomatosis, and winter scab can all be fatal, with the scab causing epizootic diseases.

Disturbance, avalanches, and other climatic accidents can also negatively impact their numbers. The maximum theoretical rate of increase is 23 to 25 percent, or 15 percent with management through hunting.

CULLING RULES RECOMMENDED IN FRANCE

Class 0 (kids): 10 to 20 percent. Priority given to sick, deficient animals, orphans at the end of summer, and others with inadequate coats at the end of November.

Class I (juveniles): 40 to 50 percent. Selective criteria are the same as for kids.

Class II (four to nine years): 10 percent. These are the best reproducers. In theory, only disabled and sick animals are eliminated.

Class III (over nine years): 30 percent. These can be recognized by their slumped spine and solitary behavior.

Barren females have horns that can grow considerably longer from the moment they become infertile. Take care not to eliminate a herd leader.

HUNTING THE CHAMOIS
The stalk

Sporting ethics dictate that the chamois should be hunted only by stalking. This is a very sporting activity that takes place in the hostile surroundings of the high mountains, and it demands quite a robust physical condition as well as excellent knowledge of the surrounding area and of the game animal's habits. Hunting usually begins before daylight, with a long climb bringing the hunter to a high point dominating the valley.

To surprise these animals, it is best to approach them from the peaks, as they tend to watch the lower-lying areas more closely. Once the chamois have been discovered, the pursuit begins as quietly as possible, preferably in a fair wind with the sun to the hunter's back. The chamois, lazy from a good

Binoculars are essential for hunting the chamois.

A kid, with the beginnings of small horns.

A detailed observation of the ground before trying to stalk.

morning feed, will be dozing in the shadow of a rock or shrub. During this time, the rifle is loaded, with the scope

Good binoculars must be light and strong, with high-powered object lenses for use at dusk.

sight mounted on the barrel. The shot is fired from about 110 yd. (100 m) at animals that have been clearly identified. The same cartridges that are used for mufflon are recommended.

European Moose

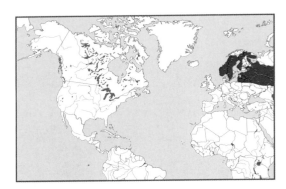

LATIN NAME:
Alces alces

The body is short and broad in the chest, with the shoulders raised in a hump. The legs are very long and strong, and the elongated head features a curiously protuberant nose. It has large ears positioned between the antlers. It is protected by a thick but short coat that forms a roll at the neck and shoulder. Under its throats hangs a hairy appendage, longer in the male than in the female. The European moose was present in Gaul during Roman times and only left Alsace in the 10th century.

The lord of the northern forests hides its outline in the most impenetrable thickets. The largest of Europe's deer, it can be found across Europe and in the countries of Scandinavia.

DESCRIPTION

The European subspecies (*Alces alces*) is confined to Russia, Scandinavia, Poland, and eastern Prussia. The male, whose body length can reach 10 ft. (3 m), and with a height to the shoulders of up to 8 ft. (2.5 m), weighs 1070 lb. (400 kg) on average – the record being around 1608 lb. (600 kg).

The moose's antlers typically take on a flat, pointed shape and can weigh up to 55 lb. (20 kg) in the European variety. These antlers are formidable weapons that are shed in the winter and grow back in spring, covered initially by protective velvet.

HABITAT

The European moose loves damp forests and marshland. Some of its physical features help it to move about on shifting ground, most notably hooves that can be planted wide apart on loose ground. Thanks to these broad hooves, many people believe that this animal is quicker than the

The female moose generally gives birth to two calves.

The fine head of a European moose.

horse. It swims happily, crossing big lakes and even arms of the sea, sometimes ending up on islands. In Russia, it was formerly forbidden to harness moose in an effort to prevent prisoners in Siberia from escaping.

DIET

The moose feeds mainly on leaves and branches, preferring willows above all. It also consumes aquatic plants for which it forages on lake bottoms.

BEHAVIOR
Reproduction

The European moose is fairly solitary. The rut takes place between the months of September and October, giving rise to a certain amount of excitement.

Unlike the stag, the male moose does not recruit a harem but only mates with females when it chances upon them.

To attract partners, the moose utters a dull bellow, audible at great distances, to which potential mates frequently respond. During this period, violent fights often erupt between large males as they charge each other and kick out with their front legs.

During the rut, the males prove very dangerous, charging with heads lowered at any intruder that comes into view, including inoffensive observers. Some moose attack trees, and others have even been seen attacking trains!

Gestation lasts for eight to nine months, and one to three calves are born at the end of spring between May and June. The females are anxious about their progeny and mercilessly remove any potential danger. Photographers must be particularly careful and keep their distance from the calves.

HUNTING THE EUROPEAN MOOSE

Hunting this animal is subject to strict legislation, and the open season generally lasts no more than a few days.

In the Scandinavian countries, the moose is hunted mainly in a battue, with hounds assisted by all sorts of fierce huskies that drive the animal back or push it toward the firing line. Stalking and ambush are also practiced.

A male feeding in a clearing.

NORTH AMERICAN
BIG GAME

Rocky Mountain Wapiti

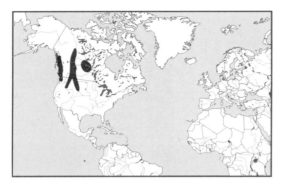

LATIN NAME:
Cervus elaphus nelsoni
or *Cervus canadensis*

The largest North American deer, living in parts of the Rocky Mountains, is sought after by most big-game hunters in North America.

The wapiti, like this one with a superb trophy head, is once again found in abundance in North America.

NUMEROUS SUBSPECIES

The wapiti is considered by most authorities to be the same species as the red deer of Eurasia (*Cervus elaphus*). There are six subspecies of wapiti in North America. These do not belong to the original fauna of the continent but immigrated there, like other European and Asian animals, when there was still a land bridge

between North America and central Asia. The most common subspecies is the Rocky Mountain wapiti (*Cervus elaphus nelsoni*), sometimes erroneously called the "elk" (which is actually another name for the moose).

DESCRIPTION

The Rocky Mountain wapiti inhabit the open forests at medium altitude during the summer. In winter, they travel down to the valleys to escape the rugged weather conditions. This animal is a solid-looking creature, bigger than the European deer and reaching the very respectable weight of 1200 lb. (450 kg). It has imposing antlers consisting of 10–12 tines, and the entire trophy can weigh up to 70 lb. (25 kg).

HABITAT

Originally, wapiti were the most widespread ungulates in North America, their habitats extending from Canada to California and Mexico. It seems that hunting was not solely responsible for the reduction in their numbers. Agriculture also played a big part in this decline, even bringing about the disappearance of

the subspecies living in the east of the country, the Eastern wapiti (*Cervus elaphus canadensis*). The deer were in fact hunted away from their winter quarters in the valleys taken over for agriculture. Constrained to spend the bad months on the snowy mountain slopes, their populations did not survive the difficult climatic conditions imposed by such altitude.

Thanks to prudent reintroduction programs beginning with stock from the Rocky Mountains and to the institution of a system of reserves (a famous one, in Jackson Hole, Wyoming, has more than 20,000 wapiti), this species has been saved from extinction. Apart from the vertical migrations imposed by the mountain climate, the behavior and biology of the wapiti are similar to those of its European counterpart.

HUNTING WAPITI

The wapiti is hunted by stalking or ambush, and hunters are aware that the main difficulty with these two techniques lies with the animal's very suspicious nature. This deer is alerted by even the slightest suspicious noise, and it is

Hunting the large American deer sometimes requires long days walking in the mountains, which more than justifies the use of a packhorse.

endowed with a very keen sense of smell. The hunter must therefore move about the forest with the greatest care, minding the direction of the wind and knowing that if the animal is ever disturbed, it will disappear at full speed and will certainly abandon that particular territory for a long period of time.

Hunting by ambush

The ambush can be practiced during the rutting season. When the wapiti calls, it utters a roaring noise very different from that of its European cousins. It begins on a low note and goes higher in four phases before descending the scale. This habit has made it possible to develop a form of call hunting. This tricky technique can be practiced in the vicinity of a clearing or meadow. The difficulty lies in synchronizing the calls well and maintaining a certain rhythm (neither too slow nor too fast) that will not arouse the suspicion of the wapiti. The animal, replying with its raucous cry, comes nearer, sometimes silently, paying constant attention to its surroundings. There are some good calls available on the market, but you can also make your own with the help of a metal pipe or a piece of bamboo 12 in. (30 cm) long and .50 in. (1 cm) in diameter.

Hunting by stalking

The second method is to hunt the animal by stalking it in places it is known to frequent, generally the feeding areas on the forest fringes or in clearings.

Stalking is carried out at daybreak or dusk, with the hunter taking care to camouflage his progress carefully. Since the male is a large animal, it should be shot with a powerful cartridge, such as a .30–06 or a .300 Magnum.

Because stalking the animal requires many long hours – sometimes even days – on foot, packhorses are indispensable.

After the wapiti is felled, it is quartered on the spot and transported in bags specially designed for this, with the trophy being placed on the back of the horse.

A large wapiti culled on an island near the coast of Kodiak in Alaska.

Other Deer

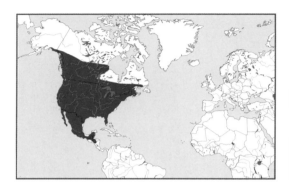

WHITETAILED DEER
LATIN NAME:
Odocoileus virginianus

MULE DEER
LATIN NAME:
Odocoileus hemionus

The mule deer and the whitetailed deer inhabit part of North America.

THE WHITETAILED DEER
Description
The whitetailed deer, also called the "Virginian deer," has a long tail that is presented like a flag once the animal has been alerted or is in flight. The deer's dimensions vary depending upon the latitude at which it lives: it can weigh more than 270 lb. (100 kg) in the Northeast, while in Florida even the largest males hardly weigh more than 95 lb. (35 kg).

Typical trophy head of the whitetailed deer, which decorates many bar rooms across North America.

Female whitetail, recognized by the absence of antlers.

Habitat

The severity of winter and the heaviness of snowfall determine the western geographical limits of this species: a snow depth of over 3 ft. (1 m) can be fatal. Despite this limitation, it can still be found in Alberta, barely 400 mi. (640 km) from the Arctic Circle. Like the roe deer, it prefers a varied countryside with some agricultural presence, but also woods and stands of trees alternating with clearings and young copses.

Diet

This deer's dietary regime is varied and includes scrub and woody vegetation in winter. In spring, it enjoys herbaceous plants, buds, and other tender shoots. Later in the year, it eats a lot of berries.

Behavior

Reproduction

The rut begins at the end of October, giving rise to furious fights between males. Between one and four young are born in the spring season of the following year.

Migration

Like many North American deer, the whitetail goes on seasonal migrations that can take it as far as 125 mi. (200 km) into the region between its summer and winter areas.

A distrustful animal

The whitetail is a solitary animal that also lives in small family groups when the weather is good. In winter, several herds may get together and form larger groupings. It is an extremely distrustful animal, so timid that, wherever it is hunted, it resolutely adopts nocturnal behavior.

THE MULE DEER
Description

From 3 to 7 ft. (1 to 2 m) long and weighing sometimes more than 400 lb. (150 kg), the mule deer is recognizable chiefly by its very long ears, for which it is named. In a large adult male, these can reach 12 in. (30 cm).

A fine double bag of whitetailed deer killed in Alaska.

Other Deer

Some ten subspecies of mule deer are recognized, of which two are relatively abundant: the Columbia mule deer (*Odocoileus hemionus columbianus*), whose distinctive antlers are in the form of a cluster of points, and the Rocky Mountain mule deer (*Odocoileus hemionus hemionus*), which is the larger animal (with a most beautiful trophy) and can weigh up to 480 lb. (180 kg).

Another subspecies worth mentioning is the Sitka deer (*Odocoileus hemionus sitkensis*), which is distributed further north along the Alaska Panhandle and the Queen Charlotte Islands.

Habitat

The mule deer, sometimes also called the black-tailed deer, is found chiefly in mountainous regions, where it may climb as high as 8200 ft. (2500 m), returning to the valleys as soon as bad weather arrives.

Behavior

Reproduction

The rut takes place at the end of October. One or two young are born in the spring, after a gestation period of 182 to 210 days.

HUNTING THE SMALL AMERICAN DEER

In view of their abundance, these game animals are widely hunted in North America.

Hunting by ambush

One of the most coveted game animals is the white-tailed deer, although it is very distrustful and very difficult to stalk, especially because it often moves around at night. One hunt-

Sometimes a river has to be crossed. Here the horse proves to be a valuable companion.

A fine kill made at the edge of the forest.

ing method that is very effectively employed is the ambush (located in advance and placed close to the deer's familiar paths, which bring it from its feeding ground at dawn to its resting place during the day).

Hunting by stalking

The whitetail can also be stalked in uninhabited regions, with the hunter moving very slowly and as discreetly as possible in the tracks left by the animals. It is then possible to discover deer slumbering in small, sunny clearings. Some specialists operate in teams of two, which doubles the chances of bagging an animal after it rises to its feet and blindly advances on one of the hunters.

Hunting from a watchtower and in a battue

Deer are also sometimes hunted from a watchtower, or more bluntly in a battue, with the help of a team of beaters. The hunting style is usually the "silent thrust,"

which does not frighten the animals as they trot across the firing line. During the rutting season in the Southwest of the United States, some hunters bang deer antlers together to imitate the noise created by two males fighting. Others in very dense marshy forests use a pack of hounds to flush out animals hiding in covert.

Firing at long range

Shooting American deer must often be done at long range, which justifies the use of a special cartridge with a very flat trajectory: .270, .25–06, .243, or .30–06. If a shot appears to fail, it is always necessary to go to the point of shot and verify that the animal was not killed. In this case, a search must be undertaken, using signs left on the ground, such as drops of blood and splinters of bone.

HUNTING WITH A BOW AND ARROW

Smaller American deer are among the game most sought-after by archers. An appropriate draw-weight for a hunting bow is 60-65 pounds – for either a recurve bow or a compound bow.

North American Moose

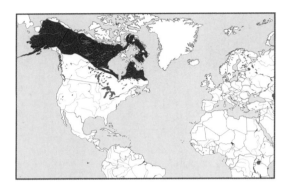

LATIN NAME:
Alces alces

OTHER SUBSPECIES

In the Rocky Mountains, you can find a smaller, paler moose: the Shiras moose (*Alces alces shirasi*), which is rarely heavier than 1200 lb. (450 kg). Two other North American subspecies should be mentioned. The Canadian moose (*Alces alces andersoni*) can be found west of Ontario, as far as the Pacific and the Beaufort Sea in the north of Alaska. It is also found in North Dakota, Michigan, Minnesota, and Wisconsin. Its range overlaps that of the eastern moose (*Alces alces americana*), which lives in eastern Canada and in some isolated locations in New England, where it survives in small numbers.

BEHAVIOR

The American moose have much the same behavior pattern as do their European counterparts, though with more pronounced aquatic habits. They rarely frequent places other than marshy forests, feeding avidly on submerged grasses. They are excellent swimmers,

The most formidable subspecies of North American moose is without doubt the Alaskan moose (Alces alces gigas), which can weigh as much as 2150 lb. (800 kg) and has extraordinary antlers in excess of 110 lb. (40 kg). This superb trophy is formed by two large "paddles" terminating in impressive tines.

DESCRIPTION

The Alaskan moose, also called the "elk," is found in the wooded areas of Alaska, eastern Yukon, and the northwest of British Columbia.

This quarry is secretive and quite unpredictable. It is considered to be one of the most dangerous game animals around, as it will charge with a rare recklessness and sometimes for no reason at all.

The charge of the moose is very impressive. Apart from the very bulk of this animal, its speed, and the formidable sight of its antlers, the visceral fear experienced by the hunter comes from the dry crash of broken trees, knocked over by this "locomotive" that nothing seems able to stop. On one occasion during the rutting season, our hunting party fired three bullets in succession with a .375 H&H Magnum, in order to stop a furious moose that had initially given no sign of such aggression.

A large Alaskan moose killed after a stalk in the brush.

North American Moose

even braving rapids, and in water they find food, refreshment, and respite from the continual attacks of insects.

More than any other animal, the moose symbolizes the strength and majesty of circumpolar wildlife. Feared by most predators, it remains a lord of the taiga, one of those rare animals that does not fear man – consequently sometimes putting its life in danger.

HUNTING THE NORTH AMERICAN MOOSE

With its most coveted of trophies, this moose is hunted widely – sometimes unreasonably so. A moose is hunted in Canada with the same ardor as a big, old wild boar in France or the legendary red deer of Germany. The pursuit is subtle, following an unchanging pattern established by the first explorers in the New World: Davy Crockett and many other trappers must have hunted the moose. The meat is firm and delicious and can be grilled at the bivouac, when the hunter is lost somewhere in the depths of the northern forest.

Moose are good swimmers. They also move with admirable agility through the densest thickets, and are endowed with a keen sense of smell and stupendous hearing.

Hunting with a call

Hunters in the United States mainly use a call, other than those in Alaska, who prefer stalking.

Hunters draw upon the ancestral techniques established by the Cree and Ojibway Indians, who used two types of call: one that mimics the bugle of the male in rut, and the other that mimics the cry of the female in estrus, which is a more plaintive and less sonorous moan. Traditional calls are made of pine or birch bark, but inexpensive techniques can be employed to make a homemade call. For example, pierce a hole in the bottom of an empty plastic bottle, and insert a piece of string. When the string is moistened and pinched between the fingers in an "off-and-on" motion, the echo chamber within the bottle will give off a dull, mooing noise.

Hunting by ambush and stalking

The moose is also hunted by ambush from a high seat or by stalking. Calibers that are generally used are the .357 H&H Magnum or the .300 Winchester.

This moose has just been quartered. Now, the large carcass is being transported on horseback. It is the end of the hunt, and the hunters are returning to camp.

Caribou

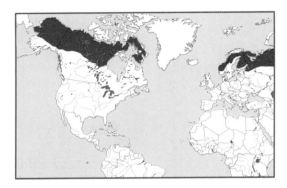

LATIN NAME:
Rangifer tarandus

Typical inhabitants of the circumpolar regions, caribou differ from all other deer in that the females also have antlers.

NUMEROUS SUBSPECIES

North American caribou are considered by most authorities to be the same animal as the Eurasian reindeer. Depending upon the country and the type of habitat they live in, there are about twenty subspecies, among them the west European caribou, the only deer to undergo domestication and the one raised by Laplanders. In Siberia, you can find the caribou of the Eurasian tundra living as far east as the Pacific coast. Another common species is the Barren Ground caribou (*Rangifer arcticus*), the most northerly variety of caribou in North America.

A fine caribou with antlers in velvet.

DESCRIPTION

The largest caribou in North America, the Osborne caribou, lives in the Rocky Mountains. It has massive, imposing antlers. This subspecies is a forest animal that rarely moves about, as opposed to the tundra caribou that migrates for more than 620 mi. (1000 km) to reach the summer or winter grounds by taking a route that never changes. This animal has exceptional endurance. Thanks to its thick fur, which is both insulating and waterproof, it can tolerate temperatures of –40°F (–40°C) without suffering from the cold. No terrain can stop it during its travels, not even when it has to cross long rivers or arms of the sea, as it swims marvelously well.

The caribou has adapted to moving about on shifting ground. The main hooves are broad, and the secondary hooves touch the ground to help to support the weight of the animal by preventing it from getting stuck in the mud.

Even today, the caribou assures the survival of numerous native peoples of North America, Siberia, and Scandinavia.

Caribou

HABITAT

Few caribou are attached to their territories, apart of course from the type that lives in Newfoundland. The inhospitable conditions of their habitat often force them to undertake long journeys, which may in fact take up an entire year.

In the heart of summer at the time of the midnight sun, caribou frequently climb high to escape the clouds of insects that flutter about the tundra. Toward autumn they come down again to more low-lying regions.

DIET

The caribou can usually fulfill its diet (based on herbaceous plants) in the tundra all summer without problems, but a thick snowfall will force it to hollow out narrow corridors with the help of its front hooves. Under the blanket of snow it finds shrubs and "caribou lichen," the basis of its winter diet.

BEHAVIOR

The caribou can weigh up to 800 lb. (300 kg), with a total body length of 8 ft. (2.5 m). The rutting period lasts from the end of summer to the beginning of autumn. After a gestation period of eight months, the females give birth in the spring. There is generally only one calf per pregnancy, although twin births are not uncommon.

A GAME ANIMAL NEEDING SURVEILLANCE

Even today, large herds of caribou are indispensable

Large caribou stalked in the tundra, north of the Arctic Circle, during an autumnal migration that brings together thousands of animals.

A superb mountain caribou shot after a march of several days in a very broken landscape.

for the lives of the peoples of western Asia and the American Far North. These animals often determine the entire fortune of the northern nomads, who are obliged to conform to the vital needs of the herds, in which the inherited migratory instinct has not been modified by man.

Across the globe, practically all caribou are subject to specific measures of protection. In the American Far North, poaching was responsible for the destruction of several hundred thousand animals around the 1950s.

It was a catastrophic reduction for the native populations of these regions, whose existence depended entirely upon caribou. These people watched out for caribou on their known routes during the great annual migrations and so

were able to capture them easily. Today, many of these natives have disappeared, along with the game that ensured their survival.

Their skins are worn by the natives with the fur side facing outward, providing good protection against the cold. The meat is popular, and the milk of females is used to make butter and cheese. The antlers, bones, and tendons are made into scrapers, knives, and other household implements.

HUNTING CARIBOU
The stalk

The most common technique used is the stalk, carried out after careful observation sessions with the binoculars. This method is not very difficult, particularly during the time of migrations.

Caribou gather in innumerable bands and take the

same route annually, which aids in locating them. A good way for the hunter to discover them is to station himself on a rise and then move cautiously downward in the direction of the herd. In Newfoundland, the forest caribou hunters track through the wood looking for separate marshy areas where they know they will be able to find an animal. It is always best to hunt in a fair wind, for the caribou is endowed with an amazing sense of smell. Any medium-powered rifle equipped with a scope is suitable, from the .270 Winchester to the .300 Winchester Magnum.

The search for meat and trophies

The meat of the caribou is much appreciated, as is the particularly remarkable trophy. Caribou antlers can be easily distinguished from those of other deer by their small size, flattened branches, pale color, and asymmetrical shape. These long, strongly curved antlers have tines right up to their extremities. The males use this impressive rack in fights with rivals during the rutting season.

Rocky Mountain Goat

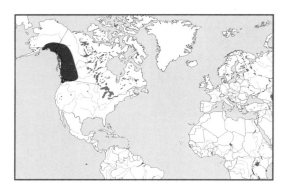

A superb mountain animal, the Rocky Mountain goat is recognized by its thick coat, made of long and very straight hairs.

LATIN NAME
Oreamnos americanus

DESCRIPTION

Both sexes have two small, tapering horns. These goats can weigh up to 360 lb. (135 kg). They are extraordinary climbers that use even tiny crags to hoist themselves up the side of a cliff. They are aided in these ascents by spongy hooves with an excellent grip,

The reward for a long and difficult stalk, as much from the nature of the terrain as from the extremely distrustful nature of the Rocky Mountain goat.

This difficult terrain is the scene of the hunt. This hunter is trying to locate the white patches that indicate the presence of a herd of Rocky Mountain goats.

allowing the goats to seem to defy the laws of gravity. The Rocky Mountain goat moves about an environment that is so steep, so hostile, and so far removed from civilization that it is commonly thought to suffer only slightly from predators. Even the wolf rarely ventures into its territory. The chief causes of death for this animal are man and accidental falls on the rocky scree.

HABITAT

Depending on climatic conditions during the year, major vertical migrations can be observed. In the heart of winter, the animals descend to seek the protective refuge of the forests, where they know they will still be able to glean a substantial amount of food. As soon as the good weather comes, the Rocky Mountain goat returns to the high peaks, which form a truly impenetrable refuge.

The Rocky Mountain goat settles in very steep areas in southern Alaska, the Yukon, British Columbia, and the Northwest Territories, as well as the Rocky Mountain states.

BEHAVIOR

The matriarchal social organization consists of several ewes, accompanied by their kids, forming flocks of around fifteen individuals. The males, however, live a solitary existence or gather in small groups that break up at the time of the rut, in November.

Reproduction

During the rut, spectacular fights occur between challengers seeking to conquer a harem. The young are born in spring, between May and June. In general, a pregnancy will produce a single kid that very quickly becomes an adept climber, moving confidently about on even the steepest slopes.

HUNTING THE ROCKY MOUNTAIN GOAT

The Rocky Mountain goat, formerly so rare that it almost became extinct, is today the subject of strict protective measures, and culls are limited.

The stalk

The very nature of the rugged terrain in which the search for the goat is carried out allows for only one kind of hunting method, the stalk. This stalk is made in very difficult conditions and demands the talents of an a mountaineer.

Furthermore, the Rocky Mountain goat remains constantly on the lookout and is very difficult to surprise. It always occupies an elevated position, remaining camped on promontories that overlook the entire valley. To surprise it, try to get around and above it to the summit of the peak.

The shot

The shot often is fired from a long range of 165 to 220 yd. (150 to 200 m) and a flat trajectory is vital. The .270 Winchester Magnum will meet the expectations of hunters stalking the Rocky Mountain goat.

North American Sheep

BIGHORN SHEEP
LATIN NAME:
Ovis canadensis

DALL SHEEP
LATIN NAME:
Ovis dalli

The Dall sheep, one of the most coveted game animals in North America.

This robust sheep, an acrobat of the peaks, can be observed as far north as Alaska.

BIGHORN SHEEP

The bighorn is a superb mountain sheep that is distributed over a vast area in North America, extending from British Columbia and central Alberta to southern California and northern Mexico.

Description

The bighorn sheep is recognized by its curved horns, making it one of the most coveted trophies of the New World. The coat generally is fawn, with lighter fur on the muzzle, hindquarters, and belly. The color varies according to the environment. Those living in the

high mountains have a paler coat than those living on the steep slopes of deserts in the south of their distribution zone. The largest individuals can weigh up to 375 lb. (140 kg).

Habitat

Like most sheep, the bighorn avoids extreme temperatures and snow that is too deep. It makes a vertical migration in winter, which may take it down from an altitude of 9800 ft. (3000 m) to one of 1600 ft. (500 m). The best winter grounds are sunny and rich in food. The bighorn returns to its kingdom in the high mountains as soon as spring arrives.

Behavior

The rut takes place from the end of October to the end of November. During this time, the largest males confront each other, the size of their horns indicating their places within the hierarchy of the herd. The female gives birth to one or

The characteristically "rolled" horns of mountain sheep.

two young after a gestation period of about 180 days.

DALL SHEEP

There are two distinct stocks: the common Dall sheep can be found in the Rocky Mountains of the Northwest Territories, Yukon, and Alaska, while

the Stone's sheep (*Ovis dalli stonei*) subspecies is found mainly in British Columbia.

Description

Dall sheep are recognized chiefly by their immaculate white coats, which make them visible at a great distance when grazing on grassy berms. They are lighter than the Stone's sheep, with fine horns that turn outward. A thick, slate-colored coat, almost black on the back, protects the Stone's sheep.

In a biological sense, the two species are perceptibly similar in their rhythms of activity to the bighorn sheep. However, they are

This magnificent Dall sheep has paid with its life for relaxing its vigilance for only a moment.

To stalk such a distrustful animal at long range is quite a feat!

less sensitive to the climatic rigors of winter.

HUNTING NORTH AMERICAN SHEEP

Because it is the most abundant, the Dall is the most hunted sheep. The hunting techniques employed are practically identical to those for the European moufflon, and that means stalking.

The stalk

Unlike for a European stalk, the terrain here is very broken and the altitudes, on average higher, require the hunter to be in good physical shape. The shot is made with a powerful, long-range cartridge like the .270 Winchester, the .30–06, the 7RM, and the .25–06.

Because of the difficulty of the stalk, a hunt for North American sheep is generally organized like a true expedition, which may last for several days. The hunters generally move on foot but are accompanied by packhorses that transport all of the necessary equipment.

The bighorn, another legendary big-game animal.

North American Bears

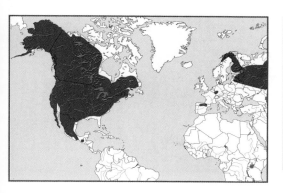

GRIZZLY
LATIN NAME:
Ursus arctos

BLACK BEAR
LATIN NAME:
Ursus americanus

POLAR BEAR
LATIN NAME:
Ursus maritimus

The grizzly bear, a legendary animal with frightening features.

On the North American continent, the great Ursidae family is represented by two main species: the grizzly, also called the brown bear, and the black bear.

THE GRIZZLY

Several subspecies can be distinguished among the grizzly, including the Kodiak (*Ursus arctos middendorffi*), a giant of the group that is confined to the island of Kodiak. This largest of living land carnivores, also called the Alaskan brown bear, can measure almost 13 ft. (4 m) when standing upright and weigh more than 1600 lb. (600 kg).

Habitat

The distribution zone of the grizzly includes the mountains of Wyoming, Montana, Idaho, British Columbia, and Alberta, extending westward to the Northwest Territories, the Yukon, and Alaska.

Diet

The grizzly exploits all natural resources during the course of the seasons. Soon

The grizzly, an opportunistic carnivore, loves eating shellfish and crustaceans on beaches.

Bears adore water. They are also without equal as swimmers and fishers.

after it wakes from a long hibernation in spring, it favors meat and consumes young mammals, such as deer calves. Then the time of plenty arrives, with massive numbers of salmon returning to the rivers from the sea. Camped in the waters, often downstream from a waterfall, the bear captures the large fish with a rare skill, using a single, quick blow of the paw. Then it makes a real mess, nibbling off several chunks from the first catch before promptly abandoning it to return to fishing. When autumn arrives, the grizzly gorges with various berries taken from the mountainside, notably blueberries. It collects them by using its claws as a kind of comb.

A discerning – and greedy – eater, it loves going for long rambles along the beaches bordering the Pacific to collect shellfish and crustaceans. It scratches the ground furiously to flush out prairie dogs and other rodents, and some have even been seen gathering whole mouthfuls of aquatic insect larvae while swimming about. A great predator, it will not hesitate to attack large prey such as deer, caribou, moose, or sheep, including scavenging the carcasses. It also, of course, loves to eat the honey of wild bees.

Behavior
The female grizzly gives birth to two or three cubs, which she will jealously watch over for the next three years. After this time, the young are abandoned, while the mother once again goes into estrus. Many naturalists claim that irascible old males sometimes kill cubs in order to enjoy the favors of a female. As soon as they are abandoned, when they weigh 400 to 540 lb. (150 to 200 kg), the young bears enter a critical phase. They are still poor hunters and are not above venturing into fishermen's camps to stealing provisions.

THE BLACK BEAR
The black bear is smaller than the grizzly and weighs a maximum of 560 lb. (250 kg). It is distributed over a large part of North America but does not occupy habitats as varied as the grizzly.

Habitat
It likes to make its home in dense thickets or in mixed forests of conifers and broadleaf trees.
Grizzlies and black bears hibernate within a lair for varying periods. In very cold regions, such as the Yukon or Alaska, this period of lethargy can last as long as six months.

Diet

Although the grizzly has a bad reputation for attacking people, experience proves – as do the statistics – that the black bear can actually be much more dangerous (not through inborn aggressiveness as much as through simple greed). This "teddy bear" consumes everything within its reach with the same gusto: animals, vegetables, and trash in

All summer long, salmon is on the daily menu of all the bears.

trashcans. It regularly raids trappers' cabins in the forest, breaking in the most solid doors when it is determined to enter, before guzzling anything sweet, including alcohol. When a bear "visits" a house, it always leaves an apocalyptic spectacle of devastation in its wake, especially when the whole bear family has joined in.

Other subspecies

About twenty subspecies of grizzly are recognized, mostly so close in resemblance that the importance of the distinction is merely

When autumn comes, the grizzly goes to the mountains to stuff itself with berries.

academic. The Kermode bear, also called the "ghost bear" because of its pale fur, can be found in the north of British Columbia and sometimes Alaska. There are also bears whose coats vary from pure black to pale honey, which can be encountered from central Mexico to the northern half of Alaska, and from the Atlantic to the Pacific.

THE POLAR BEAR

This bear can occasionally grow larger and heavier than the giant Kodiak, weighing up to 1875 lb. (700 kg). Covered in a thick, whitish coat, its elongated body makes it a swimmer without equal as well as an indefatigable walker.

This impressive black bear was shot in an ambush in the taiga near Anchorage, Alaska.

A small family looking for its daily meal of seal.

Habitat

The polar bear is a circumpolar animal, with the principal distribution zone following the entire northern maritime fringe of the continents. When the sea is frozen over in winter, it sometimes undertakes long migratory journeys in search of food.

Diet

The polar bear is a formidable predator that has an almost exclusively carnivorous diet. Its basic food is the seal, for which it patiently lies in wait near air holes and which it then captures with a rare skill. In the northern regions, polar bears make best use of the opportunities offered in the

The polar bear does not hesitate to venture onto floating blocks of ice. It can drift about like that for days, feeding mainly on seals.

month of August by the arrival of migratory arctic char. They also eat carrion, such as grounded whales, and even small rodents and birds nesting on the ground with their broods. The polar bear's only enemy is man – only Inuit, who live in the traditional manner, are allowed to hunt it (see panel).

Behavior

Like most bears, the polar bear is a solitary animal that meets possible partners only in the mating season, from June to July. The female gives birth to two cubs in a hole hollowed in the snow or ice, about 240 days after conception. The cubs are born very small and weigh only 2.5 lb. (1 kg), or 0.2 percent of their adult bodyweight. They remain sheltered for many months in a lair which, though icy, nevertheless isolates them from the bitter Arctic cold. Then the cubs begin their apprenticeships in life for a period of two years, by going hunting with

THE INUIT, THE ONLY HUNTERS OF THE POLAR BEAR

The polar bear is now under the protection of the United States Marine Mammals Protection Act, which forbids its being hunted on United States territory and also bans the import of any trophies. However, there is tolerance for the Inuit, who practice a very limited form of hunting with the help of their sled dogs – malamutes or huskies – which fiercely corner their game. Formerly, the Inuit hunters did not hesitate to confront the predator with cold steel, using a simple knife with an ivory blade.

their mothers. After this time, however, they are abandoned.

HUNTING BEAR IN NORTH AMERICA

Whether the hunt is for the black bear or the grizzly, several methods can be utilized, according to the type of country.

Stalking

Stalking is the most sporting method and is still no doubt one of the most prized procedures. It is practiced mainly in autumn and is essentially focused on the grizzly as it ventures out from cover on the mountainside to feed on blueberries. This is a particularly difficult kind of hunt, because bears have an exceptional sense of smell and excellent hearing that com-

pensate for weak vision. Discretion in the approach and many hours of marching are the keys to success.

The ambush

The black bear may be hunted by ambush, carried out from a watchtower near a charnel containing the remains of fish and the bones of moose, for example.

The weapon employed is generally a rifle equipped with a scope, such as a .30–06, a .375 H&H, or a .300 Winchester Magnum. For shooting at short range, specialists also like the drilling, with its rifled barrel in the 9.3 x 74R cartridge. When after a bear, some hunters also use a 70 to 75 pound draw weight bow or a large-caliber revolver, such as the .414 Casull.

Hunting with hounds

Some hunters, using a Scandinavian manner, hunt bear with hounds. The tactic is to corner the bear and kill it outright, which can be very dangerous for the pack.

The bear can be hunted by ambush, from a tree or high seat. To attract the animal, hunters usually put down carrion for it, consisting of meat and fish remains.

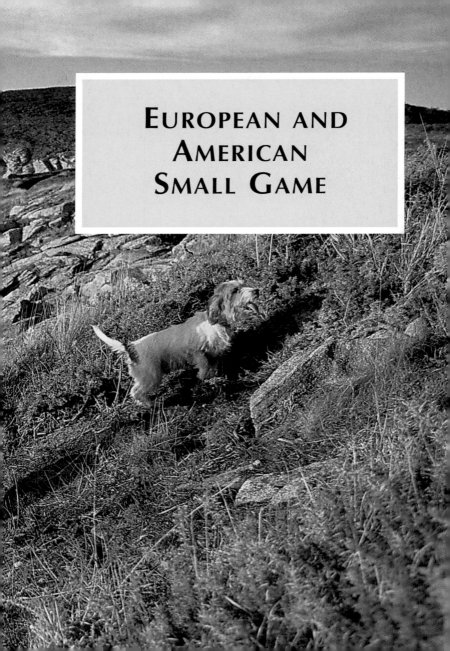

EUROPEAN AND
AMERICAN
SMALL GAME

Rabbit

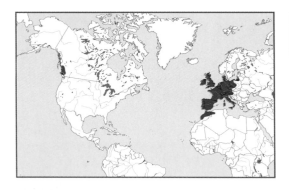

LATIN NAME:
Oryctolagus cuniculus

The well-known silhouette of the rabbit, out foraging.

Sometimes hated to the point of extermination, at other times revered by lovers of fine hunting with hounds, and often cited as an example of extraordinary fertility, the rabbit leaves no one indifferent.

DESCRIPTION

Rarely weighing more than 4 lb. (1.5 kg), the rabbit has a squat shape with legs much shorter than those of the hare. It has a gray-beige coat (although domesticated rabbits display a dazzling array of coat colors and patterns) and ears that are long but do not reach the end of the muzzle when folded. This is a lively animal, always on the alert. When it bolts, the white spot on its tail bobs up and down as if on a spring. In the weak light of dawn or evening, this is the only visible part of the rabbit.

HABITAT

Despite a strong instinct for forming colonies, rabbits never settle anywhere by chance. Exposure seems to play an important part in the decision, because warrens are often exposed to the rising sun, benefiting from good light for a large part of the day. Sandy soils and areas with excellent drainage are selected for digging out a warren. In addition, rabbits can only dig long networks of tunnels if the soil is light and crumbly. This is why rabbits are found in unlikely places (such as highway embankments, airfields, and building sites).

The rabbit, like many rodents, lives concealed in a burrow.

DIET

The rabbit has a solid appetite and will eat almost anything, such as wild grasses, legumes, young bramble shoots, aromatic plants, shrubs, and cultivated plants. Even vines, alfalfa, cereals, young fruit trees, and flowers are regular targets. This voracious appetite has caused the deepseated hatred that many farmers feel for the rabbit. The myxomatosis virus was imported into France for the sole purpose of eliminating rabbits, but no one suspected that the disease would spread through a large part of Europe.

An increasing scarcity of the rabbit in certain countries has been responsible for heavy pressure upon other species of small game animals, which unfortunately are far less prolific.

BEHAVIOR

The rabbit matures sexually very early – six months for the female and one year for the male – and has a gestation period of about one month. Some females are regularly pregnant six times a year. It's not difficult to calculate – provided there

Characteristic pose of a rabbit on the alert, near the mouth of its burrow.

Rabbit

A HOME LOVER

The rabbit rarely ventures far from its warren, most of the time less than half a mile from the place where it was born. Even when pursued by a dog or a predator, the rabbit rarely chooses a bold course of action, but rather attempts to lay a confusing scent and to return to the burrow as quickly as possible. However, very hot weather will sometimes cause an entire colony of rabbits to leave their homes and find a hillside that is more refreshing. As soon as the temperature drops in autumn, the colony returns to its familiar quarters.

are no epidemics – how quickly a sizable rabbit population can form! With such large numbers, it is easy to locate rabbits, thanks to the obvious signs of their presence: the heaps of droppings and the small depressions that they hollow out are difficult to miss. In countries where disease has not kept its population in check, the rabbit is so abundant that it is considered a pest and can be hunted throughout the year. However, it seems impossible to decimate a rabbit population by hunting alone!

HUNTING RABBIT
Hunting with hounds
Although rabbits spend a good portion of the night away from the warren, they can also be found outside in the morning and early evening. Rabbit hunting is

A young rabbit, marked as a target by many predators.

carried out by two or three hunters accompanied by two or three dogs, sometimes more. Often small but very active, these dogs are of varied breeds (such as the basset, dachshund, griffon, springer spaniel, and cocker spaniel). The dogs' role, after tracing the rabbit, is to follow the scent. Then, they are released with much vocal encouragement from the hunters. Positioned in strategic places (paths, clearings, or the borders of a hedge), the hunters follow the progress of the hunt by listening to the barking. The hunters must maintain complete silence, as the rabbit may frequently stop to listen, ready to turn back at the slightest suspicious noise. Even if the rabbit presents itself quietly, it is likely that the hunter will see it take off like a rocket. Firing should thus be instinctive and quick, and heavily choked guns should be avoided.

The fawn basset from Brittany is an excellent rabbit hound, rugged and brave in brambles.

Hunting with pointers

Rabbits have a strong natural tendency to take flight when danger occurs. However, some opt not to move at all. When blessed with warm weather, rabbits might sleep soundly in the hollow of a thick bush. These are perfect opportunities for pointers to blockade the game effectively. Rabbits can be caught easily in hedges or in the area around thick bramble bushes. Land consisting of immense, semi-barren plains also offers good opportunities, because it lacks an abundant food supply and the rabbits will forage far away from their

Copses are prized by rabbit hunters who have hounds to help them.

Rabbit

warrens. All pointers are interested in rabbits – sometimes too much so, for some tastes – but you have to make sure they do not chase after them as a matter of course, or you risk spoiling their soundness when suddenly faced with birds taking off.

Ferret-hunting is lethally effective and therefore should not be practiced during the mating season.

HUNTING GROUNDS
England and Wales

In England and Wales, rabbits are regarded as a major agricultural pest. They are hunted with shotguns, .22 rimfire rifles and also air rifles. Often, rabbits are shot at night from a vehicle using a powerful light. This is a very effective method, but great care needs to be taken to ensure that people or livestock are not shot by accident. Ferreting is also very popular and rabbits are trapped and snared. A small number of hunters still practice the highly skilled and traditional art of long netting.

Scotland

Scotland is swarming with rabbits that were largely spared from disease, thanks to strict health regulations. They can be found in copses and in fields, but it is on undulating hills covered with heather that rabbit hunting is the most interesting. Their numbers are such that hunters capture them equally well with flusher dogs (springer and cocker spaniels) or pointers. Though their numbers are great, shooting rabbits is quite tricky because they dart about ceaselessly between bushes or disappear into the slightest hollow in the ground.

This kind of habitat is marvelously suited to rabbits living in warrens.

Ireland

The rabbit is omnipresent in about half of southern Ireland. It can be found in woods, in fields, on hill-sides, and in every hedge. Kerry, Mullingar, Athlone, and the Suir River valley offer marvelous prospects. Essentially, rabbits are hunted with dogs that are good in the undergrowth and brave in brambles. They are hunted in Ireland mainly by foreigners who find them there in numbers they have never encountered before. In the marshlands around peat bogs and on the hills, the hunter will often have a chance of catching great quantities of rabbit and hare in quick succession.

Spain

Near the center of the south of Spain, the land is covered with thin vegetation, and rabbits are forced to venture far from their warrens. When danger threatens, they prefer to take refuge in a ravine or in clumps of thorn bushes. This is a chance for hunters with pointers to indulge in some wonderful hunting. In view of the warm, dry climate, bear in mind that some breeds (like the French pointer or the pointer) are more effective than setters.

France

Despite the ravages caused by the myxomatosis virus, many French regions (such as Brittany, Auvergne, Limousin, and the Mediterranean backcountry) once again have splendid rabbit populations. Depending upon the land, hunters look for rabbit by patrolling hedges and copses, accompanied by lively dogs that are not afraid of thorns, such as the cocker spaniel. In areas covered by scrub or forest, rabbits are often sought out by small, stubborn hounds that make this kind of hunting very passionate.

Some hunting teams use ferrets to dislodge the rabbits from their warrens. All known exits are then closely guarded by the shooters, who must keep their composure as well as prove their skill to take out a few rabbits.

The springer is a great dog for hunting rabbits in the undergrowth.

Brown Hare

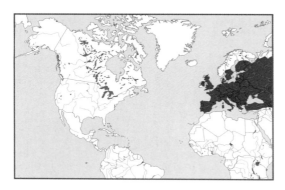

LATIN NAME:
Lepus europaeus

When a hunter says that he has a hare in his game bag, other hunters look at him with envy. The brown hare is the greatest of the small game, the coveted prize, and the prospect of a dinner among friends. The behavior of the hare is puzzling, which suggests to some that it occasionally is stupid but at other times is extremely cunning.

DESCRIPTION

The novice often declares that the brown hare is like a big rabbit, which is like saying that a horse is like a big donkey. Even if its general shape does recall that of the rabbit, there are many distinctive signs to help avoid confusion. Relatively speaking, the ears of the hare are larger and reach the end of its muzzle when folded forward. In addition, the hare's legs are much longer – especially the rear ones – and its bounding is more pronounced. The colors of its coat usually vary between russet and beige, but it may be brown or black. The belly and underside of the tail are white, while the ends of the ears are touched with black.

HABITAT

The hare lives in all sorts of environments, from cultivated plains to woods and from scrubland to mountain. It can even be found at altitudes of more than 6560 ft. (2000 m) and from fallow land to copses.

Typical confrontation between males during the mating season.

This hare is protected from the cold by a bushy cover.

The hare is a solitary animal, except during the mating period. Unlike the rabbit, the hare does not dig a burrow but lives in a form for most of the day and is mainly active at dusk and at night. The form is simple and its construction depends upon the current climate. Some forms include ferns, tunnels of green grass, bramble hedges if the temperature is mild, hollows among stones, fallen trees filled with dried grass, or thick bushes if it is colder or damp. The hare shares a large territory with other hares.

DIET

The hare's diet is essentially vegetarian and includes grasses, leaves, and grain. Vegetables are a great attraction for the hare, and it also likes aromatic plants and the bark of young trees.

BEHAVIOR

The male is polygamous, and therefore in heightened competition with others in its sector. This causes great chases that involve as many as ten individuals, some-

Hare feeding near a cabbage field.

SPECTACULAR VARIATIONS IN SIZE

The size of hares varies considerably in different places. This is true from Spain to Hungary and from England to the Ukraine. A hare from Bulgaria or Romania may reach a weight of 19 or 20 lb. (7 or 8 kg), while those in France rarely weigh more than 13 lb. (5 kg). In Spain or Ireland, a hare of more than 8 lb. (3 kg) is considered a very fine animal. Hare size depends upon the abundance of food, as is obvious from recorded differences in weight within the same country. For example, hares in the north of France weigh on average 4 lb. (1.5 kg) more than those in the southern half of the country, where the availability of food is generally poorer.

Brown Hare

Camouflaged pelts provide effective protection for leverets.

times more, and the brawls that ensue are often very violent. When fighting, hares sit up on their hind legs and look as if they are boxing. The male that has beaten its rivals gets to couple with the females, some of which reach sexual maturity a little after six months of age. After a gestation period of about 40 days, a female gives birth to two to four leverets, which are born with use of all of their senses. The female often carefully moves them to different places, to limit the risk of predation. The leverets stop suckling at three weeks old and quickly become independent.

HUNTING THE HARE
Hunting with hounds

Bringing in hounds to chase the hare is without a doubt the most spectacular method and the one that arouses the most emotion. The dogs are carefully chosen according to the landscape. Quick, medium-sized dogs, such as the French Ariégois or the Jura bruno, are used for scrub-land and the edges of open country. In areas full of undergrowth, smaller dogs that are brave in the thorns, such as the fawn basset

DISCONCERTING BEHAVIOR

The reactions of a hare in the face of danger are often unpredictable. Humans, dogs, and predators can sometimes cause the hare to take flight when they are still far away. At other times, hunters have to walk right on top of it before it will move. Crouching in a furrow in a plowed field, the hare sometimes allows itself to be observed for many minutes when it is exposed. Sheltering in the heart of an impenetrable thicket in a wood, it suddenly leaps, making the hunter jump because he did not notice it. Often it is the attitude of a hunter that seems to dictate the hare's behavior. A quite conspicuous hare will often choose not to move as long as the hunter does not look at it. When hunted without a dog, the hare will suddenly leave its cover the moment the hunter stops walking.

from Brittany or the petite basset griffon Vendéen, are used. In the morning, the lead hunter arrives with the dogs on leashes at the area around the hare feeding grounds (meadows, arable land, clearings, and the edges of woods), looking out for the slightest favor-

able sign. After the hare's entry to the form has been identified, the other hunters withdraw and position themselves near known or probable pathways. The dogs utter a few yelps once they are on to the scent of the shelter, but as soon as the animal is flushed, their

Brown Hare

THE BLUE HARE

In France, the blue hare (*Lepus timidus*) is also called the "variable hare" because it changes the color of its coat according to the season. Its coat is gray-brown in summer and scattered with white hairs in autumn. It finally turns totally white in winter, except for the black tips of the ears. The blue hare is smaller in size than the brown hare. On average, it weighs about 7 lb. (2.5 kg), and it has a more squat form, halfway between those of the rabbit and the hare. As with the brown hare, its existence is both crepuscular and nocturnal, and it shelters for a good part of the day. When snow lies thick upon the ground, the blue hare insulates itself from the cold by digging a small tunnel under the snow. The habitats of the brown hare and the blue hare regularly overlap, and from time to time, the two species mate with each other, although the resulting hybrid offspring are sterile. The blue hare can be found throughout the Alps, in Scotland, Ireland, Scandinavia, and across northern Europe.

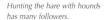

Hunting the hare with hounds has many followers.

cries come much closer together. Then, the hare is away and will probably rush at any moment toward one of the guns. Despite all preparations, a wise hunter knows that he must be vigilant as soon as he reaches his position – it is not uncommon for the hare to present itself very quietly, well before the arrival of the dogs. Sometimes the animal arrives slowly and leaves the hunter plenty of time to take aim. At other times, it stops at the edge of the covert and then bounds quickly away. This situation requires fast reflexes and coolness to successfully shoot the hare.

The battue

In open country, on immense moors, or in open scrubland, the battue is a favorite method of hunting hare. A large number of beaters is required, for hares keep low and do not bolt unless they feel that they have been discovered. A hare might leave its hiding place if the hunter suddenly freezes. However, some hares do not move when the beaters go by, and many turn back in the opposite direction to the line of the guns. At some battues, many of the beaters carry guns but will fire only at animals that turn back. The hunters in position do not usually have much difficulty with hares that present themselves at a moderate speed.

Hares that skim along close to the hunters and then sweep like a whirlwind past the firing line, darting and diving, are more difficult. The hare is sometimes shot at long range, with No. 4 shot being used. Although at times considered un-sporting, the battue does allow culls to be counted with precision and thus stimulates good manage-ment. Much land is hunted only two or three times a year by battue and not by any other method.

Hunting with pointers

Hunters do not make a specialty of using pointers very often, but those who do may flush a hare at any time. Although used more often for seeking out birds, all breeds of pointer enjoy hunting game animals. On the other hand, only land rich in hares can provide the dogs the true experience of this type of game, parti-cularly in teaching them the special places where hares

The battue in open country.

HUNTING ON FOOT

In Great Britain and France, the hare is sometimes hunted with dogs but without guns. The hunt organizers use a pack of hounds that often consists of beagles or harriers. The hare knows a lot of surprising ruses, and the pack has to work hard to catch it, succeeding only once every four or five outings. One important thing to remember is to take the hare as late as possible, so that the dogs can hunt it long enough to demonstrate their abilities when faced with tricky game.

Brown Hare

make their shelters. The Continental breeds (French pointer and spaniel) are more inclined to hunt hare than are the British breeds (setter and pointer). However, this often depends upon training and the abundance of game. Unless they are trained by their masters to hunt only one type of game, all pointers can scent and catch hare. Some intelligent dogs that are also good at pointing pursue hares when they slip away before the master has arrived, with the specific aim of making the hares come within gun range. The hunter who uses a pointer often comes across a hare while he is looking for partridge and pheasant in plowed fields, at the foot of hedges, or in a forest. When it is damp or freezing, the best places to find hare are on stony ground and on slopes facing south, where the vegetation is shorter and drier. Firing at a hare, especially in a copse, is often instinctive, because the animal springs up and is quickly covered by vegetation. At short and medium ranges, it is better to use No. 6 or No. 7 shot. Otherwise, it is better to use No. 4 or No. 5 shot, especially on the plain or in scrubland.

The hare likes sheltering in arable land and in the plains, where it is hunted in line with a pointer.

After a spaniel pointed it, this hare was taken by the first shot.

Typical hare-hunting scene in a Polish forest.

PLACES TO HUNT

Spain

Hare are abundant over a good portion of Spain and are regularly hunted with pointers – at the same time as rabbit – in country where red partridge are hunted only a few times a year and in a battue. The hares in Spain are generally small, between 5 and 8 lb. (2 and 3 kg), because food is scarce. These animals cover long distances when foraging, which multiplies the signs of their presence and also the chances of finding one.

Hungary

Hungary, like a number of other countries in eastern Europe (for example, the Ukraine, Bulgaria, and Poland), offers a lot of big hares. The hare is some-times hunted in line, with a group of hunters moving slowly across the plain. Hungarian hunters also practice the classic battue, and unbelievable scenes sometimes take place, as much because of the numbers of hares as because of their great size.

Ireland

The hare is abundant throughout Ireland and often lives side-by-side with the variable, or blue, hare. In general, the brown hare is found at low altitudes and in the area around meadows, while the vari-able hare prefers moorland, hills with poor vegetation, and the edges of peat bogs. Generally hunted in line, the hare often is shot during a hunt for pheasant or wood-cock, with the help of small dogs (cocker or springer spaniels) that extract it from the most impenetrable thickets and chase it while giving voice.

United Kingdom

Hares are widespread in the UK and are greatly prized game animals. They are hunted with shotguns and are also stalked with light rifles such as the .222 Remington.

Gray Partridge

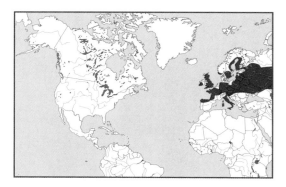

LATIN NAME:
Perdix perdix

The king of the great cereal plains, the gray partridge has suffered greatly from the modernization of agriculture.

DESCRIPTION

With its rounded shape, the gray partridge resembles a miniature chicken. Its plumage is a mixture of sober colors, with gray, brown, and russet predominating. This bird has short but powerful wings that enable it to take off quickly and make long, gliding flights. However, its most astonishing feature is how quickly it can run.

A partridge with the characteristic dark patch on the belly.

AN ENDANGERED SPECIES

The gray partridge is a dynamic bird, but many dangers apart from hunting threaten it. Predators surprise it at night (it does not roost) or in the nest, which is always easily accessible. During hard winters, half of the population may be annihilated. When this bird lives in arable land, particularly in western Europe, it is punished by modern agriculture. Coverts are rare or even non-existent, and the methods of cultivation are often fatal for broods. Insecticides indirectly kill young partridge whose dietary regime calls for a lot of insects. It is from facts such as these that hunters and farmers have drawn up agreements to improve conditions for bird life.

HABITAT

The gray partridge, also known as the Hungarian partridge, can be found in all kinds of settings, from vast cereal plains to hedged farmland, via wild meadows and hills with cropped vegetation. It only avoids enclosed places.

DIET

Fond of cereals, grasses, buds, and insects, gray partridge spend a large portion of time foraging.

BEHAVIOR

The hen lays a dozen eggs on the bare earth in a depression lined with dried grasses. She then incubates the eggs for about 20 days. From birth, the chicks

The chicks are vulnerable and often fall victim to predators, severe weather, or farming practices.

follow the adults and later form a covey. If the eggs are somehow destroyed, the gray partridge almost always lay another batch.

HUNTING THE PARTRIDGE

The battue

This favored method of hunting requires excellent organization, with no detail being left to chance. According to the wind, vegetation, and landscape, the territory to be hunted is divided into parcels that are explored one after another in a precise, chronological order. On one side, beaters walk in a line and put up the birds. On the other side is a line of guns, often arranged in an arc, toward which the birds burst forth at a lively speed. The battue requires a very special shot, and it is imperative to pinpoint the birds well before they are over the line, to make a broad and rapid sweep that compensates for their speed. The most suitable shotgun will have choke combinations of 1/4–3/4 or

Gray Partridge

1/2–full chokes. Cartridges are loaded with No. 6 to No. 7 shot, or even No. 5 on very windy days. In spite of a shooter's skill, many gray partridge are only wounded and land a considerable distance away from the point of impact. A retriever with plenty of flair and the ability to remember where several birds have fallen will help the hunter pick up all his birds.

Poland remains a renowned destination for hunting partridge.

Hunting with pointers

When hunting the gray partridge, the hunter must deal with an extensive search area. In fact, the dogs must methodically cover as much space as possible and not leave much ground unexplored. It is better to have an intensive yet less far-ranging hunt, where the dogs do not merely run but actually hunt. Gray partridge, particularly those in coveys, are constantly on the lookout and will run at the slightest provocation. The dogs must therefore be enterprising enough to get near the birds and point them efficiently. The best chances occur when the birds are isolated and the dogs are experienced enough to know how to wait for the right moment (like when the bird takes refuge in a hedge, fallow patch, or hollow). The hunter must then try, if he can make a wide detour, to come up facing the dog and give himself the best shooting opportunities. Although gray partridge take off rapidly, the hunter must still aim carefully and slowly. When a covey takes off, he must not shoot at the entire flock but rather aim at one bird and then another if he misses the first opportunity.

HUNTING PLACES
Poland

The Polish hunting grounds still resemble what many regions of western Europe looked like years ago, and gray partridge flourish there. Poland has a great diversity of habitats, with a harmonious mixture of

A courageous and effective breed, this German shorthaired pointer has gradually become the most widely kept and popular of the gundogs.

copses and immense plains. Agriculture is still "human" in Poland and remains a paradise for hunting this species. In addition, land management is well structured (maximizing reproduction, controlling predators, calculating culls, and working reserves). Tourism linked to hunting is an important resource. Practiced in large battues or sometimes in small groups with pointing dogs, hunting in Poland can fulfill all of a hunter's desires.

Belgium

Rich in small game (partridge, hare, and pheasant), Belgium is heavily cultivated, and hunting there is tightly controlled. Hunting rights to areas of variable size are put up for auction each year, and groups of hunters get together to try and acquire them.

In most places, gray partridge are hunted at the same time as other species in the course of several battues until the hunting plan is completed, which is fixed according to the size of the bird population. Other lands are hunted exclusively by drives, which are best served with good, highly obedient retrievers.

Examining the sex of the bird with a view to improving population management.

Finally, some sectors can be hunted with pointing dogs, chosen according to the landscape with a wide-ranging hunt in view.

Red-legged Partridge

LATIN NAME:
Alectoris rufa

legs and barred ocher and black on its sides. The throat is bluish-gray and is decorated with an interrupted black collar. The back and topside of each wing are duller, showing a mixture of gray and brown.

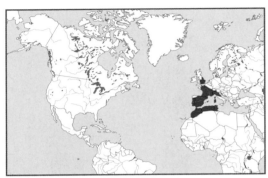

A male red-legged partridge observing its surroundings from a promontory.

A bird of scrubland, plain, and copse, the red-legged partridge is found mostly in southern Europe.

DESCRIPTION

Larger than the gray partridge, the red-legged partridge is even more generously rounded. In contrast to the gray with its sober elegance, this bird displays sparkling colors, with a bright red beak and

HABITAT

The red-legged partridge has adapted to many environments, sometimes scrubland and vineyards or the steep contours of mountains.

DIET

The red-legged partridge is indefatigable and travels far during the daytime, looking for grasses, berries, insects, and cultivated plants such as grapes, peas, lentils, and chickpeas. Partridge love places where arable land alternates regularly with coverts, open areas, and brush.

BEHAVIOR

Sometimes faithful for life, the pair establishes a nest in the hollow of a ditch, under a rock, or next to a hedge.

Running flight is a means of defense frequently used by the red-legged partridge.

is damp and they balk at leaving shelter.

Hunting in a battue
Some hunting grounds under special management (such as those in Spain) are hunted only by battue and only for a few days each season. The managers of these lands claim that it is better to disturb almost all of the birds in one area a few times per year, rather

The chicks emerge after 20 days of incubation and are closely watched as they immediately follow their parents. They then form a covey, whose social cohesion rarely breaks down. Very discerning, red-legged partridge know when to abandon hunting grounds and establish themselves close to inhabited areas, where they know there is no risk.

HUNTING THE RED-LEGGED PARTRIDGE
Hunting with pointers
Living in medium-sized groups in most of the countries it inhabits, the red-legged partridge is basically hunted with pointers. This is a rugged hunt, sometimes taking place over uneven terrain, and the dogs must possess endurance and a keen sense for hunting. The birds run very fast, using vegetation and the contours of the land marvelously well to conceal the takeoff, and they prove difficult to blockade. It is often impossible to get very close to the entire covey. Some of the best hunting occurs when the hunter seeks out the hiding places of isolated birds, either when it is warm and the partridges are digesting food or when the ground

Superb red-legged partridge shot in the Corsican maquis.

Hunting red-legged partridge with a pointer often takes a lot of effort, but it always arouses great emotions.

than the reverse. On those occasions, the hunters operate from fixed positions, while a large line of beaters drives the game toward them. The flushed birds pass at top speed over the shooters, who must have an excellent "swing" to hit these veritable meteors.

HUNTING PLACES
Spain

In Toledo, Andalusia, and many other places, Spain harbors some superb land for red-legged partridge. These habitats are particularly good for the optimal development of this species – this is one reason that many trainers arrive during January and February to train their pointers for upcoming competitions in spring. The hunting is sometimes done in gigantic battues that drive the birds toward a line of guns. Many estates authorize this kind of hunting for the red-legged partridge only, with hare and rabbit being shot by walking up. Some estates are suitable for pointers – bearing in mind the climate and the lack of water, resistant breeds like the burgos, German pointer, and pointer will be more at home there.

Fine populations of red-legged partridge can be found in France (the Mediterranean regions), Ireland, England, and also the south of Italy.

In Spain, the red-legged partridge enjoys an absolutely perfect habitat and climate.

THE ROCK PARTRIDGE

The rock partridge can be found in the mountains of the Alps and in Albania, Crimea, Kazakhstan, and other eastern European countries. Similar to the red-legged partridge, the rock partridge (*Alectoris graeca*) is distinguished by a larger size, reaching 3 lb. (1 kg) in exceptional cases. Other signs that help to identify rock partridge are the interrupted black collar and two black bars on the side feathers, as opposed to the single bar of the red-legged partridge. Rock partridge live in coveys and are even less approachable than red-legged partridge. This bird's resistance to extreme conditions – of both climate and food supply – is impressive. Sometimes the rock partridge and the red-legged partridge interbreed, especially in regions where their territories overlap.

Ring-necked Pheasant

LATIN NAME:
Phasianus colchicus

DESCRIPTION

It must be impossible not to recognize a ring-necked pheasant – even for someone who does not hunt – because its shape and colors are so characteristic. The ring-necked pheasant has a head which shimmers green and blue, red cheeks, and a pure white collar. It has a red and golden-orange body that is punctuated with white and black, and its long maroon tail is barred with black. While the cock's plumage is sumptuous, the hen is discreet and camouflaged, in a prudent mixture of maroon, beige, and brown streaks.

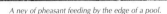

A ney of pheasant feeding by the edge of a pool.

With the regal bearing of a monarch strutting about his kingdom, with sparkling colors and a spectacular takeoff, the ring-necked pheasant embodies all of the majesty of birds. Enthusiastically hunted in many countries, it always arouses a great deal of interest, particularly in places where the populations have remained wild.

The cock is a hardy bird that is good at tolerating severe winter weather.

COUSINS THAT ARE JUST AS BEAUTIFUL

There are many species of pheasant in the world, and some have been specifically introduced for ornamental or hunting purposes, with varying results. Thus, it cannot be said that the golden pheasant (*Chrysolophus pictus*) has ever become a success, even if some birds have managed to survive in the wild. This is the same with the Lady Amherst's pheasant (*Chrysolophus amherstiae*). On the other hand, the Reeve's pheasant (*Syrmaticus reevesii*) has shown a surprising ability to adapt in areas where it has been properly managed, and it has fabulous defensive qualities while in woodland. The male Reeve's pheasant has a sumptuous pale-colored tail barred with black that is up to 6 ft. (2 m) long! The dark or melanistic pheasant is not, technically speaking, a separate species of pheasant. Rather, it is a mutation of the common pheasant, and its black plumage with metallic highlights is magnificent.

HABITAT

Like all of the gallinaceous birds, the ring-necked pheasant spends a major part of its time walking, preferably on open ground (meadows with short grass, paths, and rides), in woodland, and in fallow fields late in the day or when it has been disturbed. Ring-necked pheasant roost during the day in times of danger but also at night – and so escape predators.

DIET

The diet of this bird is varied. It eats wild berries, grapes, grains of wild grasses, and corn, as well as snails and insects. The ring-necked pheasant prefers arable lands near forests, meadows, and moorland. It also needs a lot of water and is often seen beside ponds and streams.

The wild pheasant makes life difficult for the pointer.

Ring-necked Pheasant

FRANCE'S ORIGINAL WILD POPULATION

Against all expectations, one of the finest populations of wild pheasant lives near the shores of the Var River, on Porquerolles Island in the Mediterranean. The following ingredients combine to prove the dynamic nature of the pheasant and its aptitude for colonizing a beneficial environment: a variable landscape of coverts, fallow fields, and farmland, plus control of predators, reasonable culls, and the ability to control an island habitat. Other small Mediterranean islands, in addition to those of the Atlantic, also have populations of wild pheasant.

BEHAVIOR

Just before spring, the cock utters its regular, harsh cry to announce that it will not tolerate any other males in its territory. If necessary, the cock will provoke a rival that ventures into its area, inflating its plumage to impress the other male and attacking with the beak and talons. The cock is polygamous and usually has three hens, although this number varies depending upon the surrounding resources and the ability of the male to assert its rights. Thus, it may just as easily serve three or four hens. After mating, the cock leaves each hen to raise the young, without showing any interest in its progeny. On average, 10–12 eggs are incubated for about 24 days. The chicks leave the nest and immediately follow their mothers, eating a carnivorous diet for the first weeks of life. Insects, larvae, and mollusks make up the diet, and they also

Two cocks confronting each other during the mating season.

Typical pose of a pheasant uttering a harsh cry while marking its territory.

have a great taste for ants, especially their eggs.

HUNTING THE PHEASANT
The battue

Raised to the rank of an institution, the pheasant battue is a highly prized method of hunting, with its progress often taking on a ceremonial air. A true battue for pheasant is not something to be improvised. The organizers must have an excellent knowledge of the habits of their pheasant population, and if possible should choose a time when the weather will be favorable. Either a blind, where the shooters can conceal themselves on a plain, or a row of trees make up the firing line. Each line of fire corresponds to one well-defined parcel of land, which the beaters will cover, often accompanied by a dog. Although some people say that the battue

is hardly sporting for the hunter, this type of hunting demands quite a bit of shooting skill. The ring-necked pheasant is not an easy kill once it is in the air, flying at 98 ft. (30 m) and higher. This is especially true for the hunter who is accustomed to firing at birds

while walking up and not at those flying overhead. For this special kind of shot, the hunter should not hesitate to use a moderately choked

Hunters posted in line, waiting for pheasant to be sent over by the beaters. Shooting this bird in a battue is very difficult!

Ring-necked Pheasant

shotgun (1/2 and full) and No. 6 or No. 7 lead cartridges. Bearing in mind the speed of the birds, the aiming sweep must quickly get well in front of the bird. It is also vital to memorize the number of birds shot and where they fall, as well as the direction taken by wounded birds.

Hunting with pointers

Debased in some countries where many birds are specially raised, the ring-necked pheasant is no less a proper hunting bird, and its qualities are just as good as those of the partridge and other mountain galliforms. This bird hides away at the slightest warning and runs at an incredible speed.

Experienced dogs

Dogs that hunt ring-necked pheasant must prove that they can hunt intensively and move with an air of authority while pointing perfectly. Dogs that are too cautious will have difficulty when blockading birds and often only point at places that the game has recently abandoned. Tracking dogs, like the German pointer, are useful for finding out the trace of a bird that has slipped away. On the other

WALKING UP

This type of hunting, which is frequently practiced, is a blend of the battue and shooting to the front. A group of hunters, their numbers and spacing depending upon the size and nature of the habitat, walk in a line with their dogs. This effective method demands excellent discipline and strict shooting instructions. In addition, the dogs used must use a short-distance style and be extremely obedient, particularly when they retrieve the game.

hand, a dominant dog, like the pointer, will often manage to control the game totally. Experienced dogs are enterprising only in an area full of undergrowth, giving the shooter a chance to get into a good firing position.

On the morning of the hunt, the hunters will bring the dogs close to the pheasant's feeding areas (farmland, meadows, beside hedgerows

and pools) and then widen the search to the surrounding cover.

Shooting

Shooting pheasant does not pose major problems on open land, provided that time is taken to aim carefully at the bird. This is not true for woodland or thick brush, because the cocks are quick to fly into the treetops and the hens are masters at flying low. In these cases, the hunter must fire the shot more instinctively. Medium-choked weapons, which are suitable for hunting pheasant with pointers, should be used with No. 6 or No. 7 shot, fired from between 11 and 33 yd. (10 and 30 m).

HUNTING PLACES
Poland
Hunters in Poland organize large battues over enormous areas of flat country, where farmland alternates with fallow fields and woods. A broad line of hunters shoots at the birds (and often at hare), driven by a veritable army of beaters. Some of these battues may result in the spectacle of several hundred dead birds. Moreover, some of these areas are hunted only once or twice a year. In other eastern European countries, such as Bulgaria or Hungary, hunters practice the same type of hunting but will not exclude the possibility of using pointers.

British Isles
In England, Scotland, and Ireland, pheasant is abundant and is one of the most venerated game birds. Hunts are tightly organized, and in many places are conducted only in a battue or drive. In Ireland, the pheasant is considered the king of game birds and is often hunted in woodland and on moors with the help of flusher dogs (sometimes pointers) in small groups of three to five hunters. Most of the time, only the cock may be shot, because population management relies upon the polygamous habit of the pheasant and aims to leave each area with three times as many females as males.

A fine cock retrieved by a Brittany spaniel.

Grouse

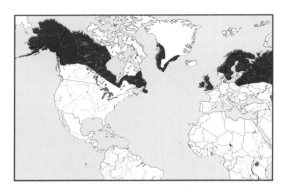

WILLOW PTARMIGAN
LATIN NAME:
Lagopus lagopus

ROCK PTARMIGAN
LATIN NAME:
Lagopus mutus

RED GROUSE
LATIN NAME:
Lagopus lagopus scoticus

Grouse are small members of the Tetraonidae family, which inhabits a good portion of countries within the Northern Hemisphere.

Hunting grouse can be either disconcertingly easy or among the most demanding of disciplines. Grouse are reminiscent of the partridge, with a rounded shape and great skill at running, coupled with a rapid takeoff and mastery of gliding flight. Although these birds have few habitat requirements, they prefer Arctic surroundings and live in the rather inhospitable countries of the Northern Hemisphere (the grouse populations of the Alps and Pyrenees are mere relics). Grouse are satisfied with a diet based on buds, grasses, and berries, and they characteristically adopt different plumage throughout the year, first gray-brown in summer, predominately white between seasons, and then pure white in winter. Only the red grouse keeps its dark plumage all year.

THE WILLOW PTARMIGAN

The willow ptarmigan can be found from Siberia to Scandinavia and in North America. A bird of the

There are several species of grouse that generally inhabit high mountain regions.

The willow ptarmigan.

lower weight, the rock ptarmigan has adapted to the worst climatic conditions, not only by donning completely camouflaged plumage in winter, but also by withstanding the lowest temperatures in the most severe habitats. These birds can be found in Iceland, the Scandinavian mountains, western Europe (where it is often called the "white partridge" or "snow partridge"), France, the Pyrenees and the Alps, the Italian Piedmont, and Switzerland.

tundra and coniferous forests, the willow ptarmigan lives in flocks throughout the year, and it is not unusual to see hundreds, even thousands, of them gathering together in the cold season. This bird's distribution area overlaps with that of the rock ptarmigan, especially in Scandinavian countries.

THE ROCK PTARMIGAN
Similar in every respect to the willow ptarmigan except for a

THE RED GROUSE
A subspecies of the willow ptarmigan, the red grouse is found only in Scotland, Northern Ireland along with a few other northern islands. Its habitat consists of moorland covered with heather and rocky hills with low vegetation where the birds feed on berries. In the extreme north of Scotland, these grouse live alongside the rock ptarmigan.

HUNTING GROUSE
In many Nordic countries, grouse are so abundant that hunting them is relatively easy.

These birds are generally hunted by a method that is a blend of rough shoot and stalking. Grouse are gregarious and are found in flocks of ten or more birds. However, danger will make them disperse, and hunting then consists of seeking out the isolated birds, rather like the way partridge are hunted.

Hunting with pointers
Practiced mainly in western Europe (in

The rock ptarmigan.

Grouse

The red grouse, the most illustrious game bird of the British.

the British Isles and the Alps), hunting with a pointer is worthy of this most renowned game bird. Grouse live in vast areas that are sometimes difficult to access, such as steep slopes that are higher than 9840 ft. (3000 m), and they must be approached very carefully. With this method of hunting, enterprising dogs – basically pointers and setters – must show endurance yet have the chance to exhibit their qualities to the fullest. The hunter has to walk for seven or eight hours in tough conditions.

In the uneven contours of the Alps or Pyrenees, hunting grouse is unquestionably more difficult than hunting the black grouse or western capercaillie (*Tetrao urogallus*).

HUNTING PLACES
North America
In North America, particularly in the southern part of Alaska, the abundance of grouse is fabulous. These grouse often are hunted at the same time as hazel grouse by searching in sparse forests, around the edges, and in clearings.

Scandinavia
In Scandinavia, where willow ptarmigan and rock ptarmigan are often found, there is no shortage of areas populated by grouse. Hunting is sometimes conducted on the tundra, in the sparse forests of small conifers, and in the mountains. According to the season, progress is

GROUSE BATTUES

Very fashionable on many Scottish estates, which often have an area of more than 24,700 acres (10,000 hectares), the grouse battue has become a great classic. It has a strongly elitist connotation, bringing together wealthy clientele and select guests for an event whose sartorial elegance leaves the uninitiated stunned. A walking line of beaters drives hundreds of birds toward a line of guns that is generally positioned in small stone towers (butts). There, comfortably installed and enjoying a broad field of vision, the shooter surveys the horizon. With this method of hunting, the grouse is seen not so much as a bird but as a target and a way of pitting one hunter's skills against those of others.

made on foot (in August and September) or on snowshoes once the snowfall is sufficiently heavy.

France and Italy

In France and Italy, especially in the Alpine massifs, grouse are generally present in average numbers and are hunted exclusively by pointer. The reverse of what happens in countries with heavy populations, hunting grouse in these areas comes closer to a sporting performance because the terrain is so demanding and the birds are so difficult.

Grouse and blue hare bagged in a rough shoot in North America.

Woodcock

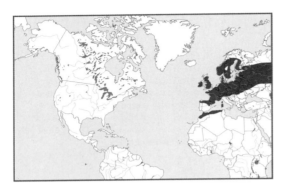

LATIN NAME:
Scolopax rusticola

With a long beak, 180-degree panoramic vision, and enormous wings, the woodcock is a unique bird. It is a long-distance traveler, with many migrations and staging posts that still remain a complete mystery.

Still sometimes called "the bronze one," this beauty of the woods has melted the heart of many a hunter.

A GREAT TRAVELER

The distribution zone of the European woodcock is vast, extending from Scandinavia to within the borders of Mongolia, passing through Siberia and all of the countries bordering the Caspian Sea, the Black Sea, the Adriatic Sea, and the Mediterranean. These migrations take it as far as North Africa, Turkey, and Iran. Naturally, all of the countries of western Europe welcome it from autumn onward or accommodate it throughout the year.

In the migratory period, woodcock may land anywhere, including in a hedge.

DESCRIPTION

On average, the woodcock weighs between 10 and 11 oz. (300 and 350 g). It has a rounded shape, and its plumage is the color of dead leaves and provides excellent camouflage. The woodcock is a wading bird equipped with powerful feet. Its wings are long and powerful, making it a bird that flies fast from the first few yards. Eyes that are positioned at the very top of the head give this bird a wide range of vision, which explains the aerial feats it performs in the forest as it flashes past all obstacles at an astonishing speed.

THE SMALL AMERICAN COUSIN

The American woodcock (*Scolopax minor*), a relative of the European woodcock, can be found over a large portion of the United States, from Louisiana to Canada. Although identical in shape to the European woodcock, the American woodcock is about one-third smaller. There are also variations in plumage, in particular a greater amount of orange and russet on the American woodcock. In daylight both types of woodcock stay in woodland, and both have the same preferences for rich, humid soil. The American and European woodcock share the same skill at flying beneath the woodland canopy (the former is lighter and can perform feats of even greater virtuosity), and both experience the same nomadic tendency as ordained by climatic changes. For hunting the American woodcock with a pointing dog, nothing that concerns either the search by the dogs or the shooting differs, except that this woodcock has a tendency to hold better than its European cousin. However, its takeoff is diabolical.

Woodcock

HABITAT

Woodcock do not inhabit just any forest, in terms of either configuration or elements. Generally speaking, uniform forests and large-scale trees do not attract many woodcock, and then mainly on the edges or in clearings. On the other hand, mixed forests and relatively young forests attract these birds more frequently.

BEHAVIOR

Outside of the breeding period and when it is migrating, the woodcock is generally a solitary bird that spends much of the day surrounded by forest or shrubs.

THE WOODCOCK AND ITS COVERTS
The daytime covert

When not on the move, the woodcock adopts an area where the trees are thinly scattered and the ground is fresh and damp, often at the edge of a forest, or near a clearing, river, or peat bog. It is curious to note how far the woodcock remains faithful to this routine, as it will sometimes spend the entire day within a radius of less than 330 ft. (100 m). Once disturbed by a hunter or a mushroom picker, this

Woodcock digging for earthworms in a meadow at dusk.

bird leaves its covert but always returns.

The nocturnal covert

At dusk, the woodcock takes off for its nocturnal covert, which is generally situated in a pasture, damp meadow, or piece of culti-

The woodcock may suffer from hard winter weather, especially when the ground is frozen deep down, preventing it from getting food.

RINGING WOODCOCK

In some countries, most notably in France, Ireland, and Great Britain, teams of specialists are actively ringing woodcock.

Capture by netting

In this nighttime operation under the control of officers authorized by hunting and wildlife protection agencies, woodcock are sought out with powerful flashlights in the wet meadows where they customarily spend the night. When the operator manages to transfix a bird on the ground with the light, a helper covers the woodcock with a wide net. Then they weigh the bird,

determine its age (by looking at the wing feathers), and attach a numbered ring to one leg.

A valuable aid for tracking populations

In the register, each ring number provides valuable information about the bird, as well as the date and place of the ringing. This is how we know that many woodcock that are culled in Ireland are sedentary, that those in Great Britain come mostly from Scandinavia, and that some in France, Italy, and Spain come from Russia. Ringing is the best means of knowing the exact distance between the zones where the birds nested and where they spent the winter, even if the routes taken on these long journeys remain unknown. Ringing has also made it possible to confirm that woodcock are faithful to their overwintering sites, as the recovery of rings just several hundred yards from where they were initially attached attests.

vated marshland, or near the edge of a river or pool. In wet ground, a long, tactile beak has no trouble picking out earthworms, which constitute 80 to 90 percent of its diet. It is thought that this nocturnal feeding period motivates the woodcock's regular movement out of the forest and in the direction of meadows and fields. The woodcock, which always lives on the ground, feels safer in open country, since it has a much better chance of seeing possible predators. Just before dawn, the woodcock leaves its foraging area and nocturnal resting area to return to a forest covert. The daytime is punctuated by phases of rest and

feeding, provided this bird is not disturbed.

HUNTING WOODCOCK
Hunting with pointers

Few birds arouse as much passion among pointer hunters as the woodcock. Hunting woodcock is magnificent, exhilarating, and wild, but also chancy, testing, and demanding. It requires total commitment and a willingness to undergo a big effort. As much for the hunter as for the dogs accompanying him, these two elements are closely bound together, since the

love of hunting and cooperation rule the man-dog partnership. All breeds of pointing dog are suitable for hunting woodcock, from the spaniel and the pointer to the Continental pointer and the setter. It is the hunter's responsibility to make these dogs specialists by hunting in woodland and by taking them out as frequently as possible. Although he must face the hazards of migration and the constant movements of the birds, the woodcock hunter is nonetheless not totally deprived of support. The weather can help him predict certain large-scale movements, especially when a cold spell hits a region with the reputa-

This young woodcock is carefully watched over by its mother.

An English setter with an electronic collar that allows it to be located when standing at the point.

tion for harboring a lot of birds. The alert woodcock hunter knows to vary his explorations from one altitude to another, in line with climatic changes. Each place where a woodcock has been flushed must be memorized, and all similar areas will then be well worth trying.

Hunting with flusher dogs and scrubland experts

In some countries, such as Ireland or Scotland, hunters often use flusher dogs (cocker and springer spaniels). Small in size, these dogs are bursting with energy and passion, and their endurance is sometimes amazing. Although they are often reproached for not pointing game, their unique way of hunting consists of listening, approaching, and forcing the bird to take off. This method of hunting is decried by some but remains attractive to others. First of all, the birds are forced to fly and cannot run far on foot,

Woodcock

The springer is much prized by Irish woodcock hunters.

and this constraint is particularly useful in places where the undergrowth is dense. It is clear that in areas where woodcock are not very wild, flusher dogs offer fewer shooting opportunities than do well-trained pointers. This is simply because the hunter does not have time to get into position or prepare himself for the bird taking off. Perhaps this is a less attractive form of hunting than other methods that use pointing dogs, but it spares quite a few birds. Although the hunter sees quite a bit of them, he shoots a significantly smaller number, and the shooting is often very

A Brittany spaniel, very proud of its two woodcock.

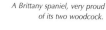

Superb point by an English setter.

tricky. On the other hand, running all day behind two or three springers on the edge of woods that border peat bogs is not without its sporting qualities. These devilish dogs are in fact very lively, and the hunter must always be alert in order to discover favorable shooting opportunities.

Courtship hunting
Decried in western Europe and forbidden for most of the time, courtship hunting is practiced in many eastern European countries and also in Scandinavia. Most of the woodcock hunted by pointing dogs in the temperate regions are born in these countries, where the best hunting periods are markedly shorter. Stretching over several months, the courtship period occurs when pairs of woodcock breed.

Morning and evening, the males fly over the forests, clearings, river banks, and moors, performing an aerial ballet whose aim is to attract females. Positioned on the edge of a forest or on a rise surrounded by woods, the shooter takes position in the morning and the evening to watch the movements of the woodcock.

The hunter is in position for an hour after sunrise and

half an hour before nightfall, and in this way he sometimes has the chance to shoot several woodcock in one day.

HUNTING PLACES
Ireland

The Emerald Isle is a paradise for woodcock, due to the damp, mild climate. For most of the hunting grounds, the hunter's chances of success are often best from the middle of December to the end of January. The areas vary from copses and small forests of broadleaf trees beside rivers, moorland, and peat bogs, to plantations of young conifers and steep hills with twisted trees and thorny bushes. Kerry, in the southwest of Ireland, offers fabulous and diverse areas, enabling the hunter to completely change his setting daily.

France

The first significant arrivals of woodcock occur two

The Brittany spaniel is undoubtedly the ancestor of all woodcock-hunting dogs.

This Irish hunting guide, always delighted at the feats of his clients, is accompanied by a Continental pointer.

20th century. However, these numbers could be due to increasing numbers of birdwatchers that keep the figures accurate and up-to-date. However, it is still true that many forested massifs (the Pyrenees, Auvergne, Savoy, Jura, and Vosges) provide sightings from September, though in very small numbers. There is a surprise awaiting the hunter who, at the beginning of October, flushes a few birds at altitudes as high as 6560 ft. (2000 m)!

Crimea

Located at the southern end of the Ukraine, from which it is now independent, the Crimean Peninsula projects

The German pointer is an excellent dog for woodcock.

weeks into October, but November and December are really the two major months for woodcock in France. All of the French *départements* are host to woodcock, but in unequal numbers. This variation in density is also accompanied by fluctuations caused by the progress of migration, which means that the average *département* shows results that vary greatly from one year to the next. The best regions are those with mild climates that are located close to the English Channel, the Atlantic Ocean, or the Mediterranean Sea. For many years, there has been a noted tendency for woodcock to settle in France, perhaps because of the regular increase in forested land – more than 30 percent during the course of the into the Black Sea. Enjoying a Mediterranean climate, the hunting grounds of Crimea are an almost obligatory staging post for woodcock flying south from Siberia and Russia. Some woodcock land at altitudes of 2620 to 3940 ft. (800 to 1200 m) from the beginning of October, on wooded land with easy access. Later, cold weather forces these birds to retreat toward the Black Sea or the Russian Sea of Azov, to settle at altitudes of 980 to 1310 ft. (300 to 400 m) on steep slopes covered with mixed forests in which oaks and pines predominate. Some woodcock spend the entire winter in these low-lying areas,

while others continue toward the coasts of Bulgaria, Georgia, and Turkey. Globally, the numbers of woodcock are truly phenomenal from October to the end of November, and it not uncommon to flush 20 to 30 birds a day with the help of two dogs.

Quebec

With its vast areas of forest and copse, Quebec is a favored destination for hunting the American woodcock. Broadleaf trees predominate in this area, and these forests harbor extraordinary numbers of birds, living side-by-side with large numbers of hazel grouse. In September, the hunting stock is composed chiefly of broods of sedentary woodcock, though finding them requires good knowledge of the locality, because some sectors are well populated while others are veritable deserts. For most of October, large contingents of migrants land everywhere in the woods bordering the St. Lawrence River. It is not unusual to flush 15 to 20 birds a day with a pointing dog.

The Woodcock is a bird that arouses the greatest passion among hunters who use pointing dogs.

Black Grouse

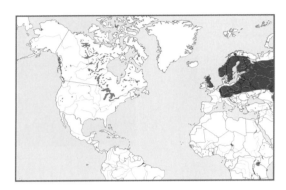

LATIN NAME:
Tetrao tetrix

DESCRIPTION

This superb mountain bird, the size of a domestic chicken, displays clear sexual dimorphism. While the female is covered by plumage in dull colors, the male in contrast wears gleaming feathers of shiny blue-black and has a red wattle and a lyre-shaped tail.

The black grouse is famous for spectacular courtship displays and is a symbol for protected or virgin habitats. Many hunters profess that the black grouse is a dream bird. This is because the hunt for the "black prince" over wide-open spaces is always touched with magic!

Male black grouse, ready to do battle in the breeding season.

A boggy area, much favored by the black grouse.

HABITAT

The black grouse can be found in varying numbers from the mountains of the Alps to the steppes of Kazakhstan, via the moorlands of Scotland and the vast lands of Scandinavia. If you were to compile a list of the different landscapes within the areas inhabited by the black grouse, you would notice that this bird needs space, particular foods, and tranquility. In France, where it is categorized with other mountain galliforms, the black grouse is not found in satisfactory numbers except above altitudes of 5250 to 5900 ft. (1600 to 1800 m) and only in areas difficult to access.

The black grouse above all needs diversity, a mixture of coverts and open areas. In places where it is overhunted or disturbed by tourist activities, the black grouse almost always takes refuge in the most wooded parts of steep slopes, although it has more than one refuge area. While enjoying plenty of peace and quiet, the black grouse visits open places, such as copses, the upper levels of forests, and rolling plains. In fact, it is in these types of country that this bird finds the essentials of its diet.

Courtship parade: two cocks confront each other.

DIET

The diet consists of buds, seeds, berries, and leaves. In winter, the black grouse often digs a shelter in the snow to insulate itself from the cold, and it eats lichens, pine needles, tree barks, and fruits that have been preserved by the cold.

HUNTING THE BLACK GROUSE
Hunting with pointers

In western Europe, the black grouse is sought out mostly by hunters with pointers. Pointers and setters (chiefly the English and to a lesser extent the Gordon and the Irish) are

Black Grouse

Hours of walking in the French Alps were needed to put this black grouse in the bag – but what a reward!

most highly prized for their long-range abilities and the extent of their flair. Although a few Continental breeds (some strongly infused with English blood), such as the Brittany spaniel, the German pointer, and the drahthaars, do not cover much ground, they are efficient when tracking and retrieving.

A long and meticulous quest

Conducted with only two or three hunters (after that, it becomes a battue), hunting with pointing dogs consists of exploring the feeding areas facing south or southeast that are located at the upper limit of the forest in the morning. Generally, these birds are on the lookout and are difficult to surprise in these open areas. At noon when it is warm near the crests or at the top of wooded slopes facing north, the chances of a definite point are significantly greater. For the rest of the day, the birds must be sought on the steepest slopes and close to uneven ground. This exceptional form of hunting requires excellent physical condition and a good mental state, for both the dogs and the hunters. As a rule, the hunter will walk for eight to ten hours on very uneven ground in exchange for a few shooting opportunities.

Shooting

The black grouse is a good runner, and most hunters rarely get in a shot at close range. You must try to get below the dog or detour around and come up facing it. For fast and instinctive shooting, it is clearly an advantage to have a handy, light gun (choked 1/4 and 3/4). The black grouse is a solid bird, and cartridges loaded with No. 5 to No. 7 shot are needed for it.

Stalking

Black grouse are stalked in Scandinavia and several eastern European countries. Stalking is a sporting method, particularly when there is snow on the ground and progress on snowshoes or skis is hard. It can become extremely difficult for the hunter to conceal his presence. Of course, the hunter tries to spot the birds from afar with binoculars, to make the best use of vegetation when disguising his approach. For an effective shot, it is ideal to find birds up in the trees. It is better to use a rest for aiming, such as a backpack or stalking stick. From the side, aim between the joint and the white part of the wing. When front-on, aim at the breast between the tops of the wings. Choose a light, small-caliber rifle, preferably equipped with telescopic sights, because it is difficult to clearly see a bird several dozen yards away.

HUNTING PLACES

All of the countries that are crossed or bordered by the Alps harbor the black grouse, but actual numbers vary. The birds are generally found above 4590 ft. (1400 m) on rough terrain. The Scandinavian countries and Scotland have rather good populations of black grouse, which live alongside the western capercaillie and the rock ptarmigan in accessible areas.

Many eastern European countries are a true paradise for black grouse, but it is in the vast region of Kazakhstan that the largest numbers of black grouse on the planet can be found.

Living in variable numbers from one country to the next, the black grouse is still a true trophy bird.

Spruce Grouse

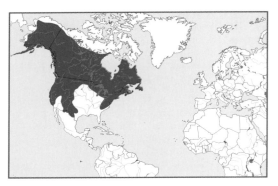

LATIN NAME:
*Dendragapus
canadensis*

DESCRIPTION
The spruce grouse, also called the Canadian grouse, looks like a grouse in every respect.

HABITAT
This bird is most often found in Canadian conifer forests, such as those in the Natashquan basin in Quebec, where it is abundant and disconcertingly familiar.

*There are a number of subspecies grouped under the **Tympanuchus** genus whose behavior and feeding habits are very similar. A bird of plain and copse, the spruce grouse inhabits the northern part of the United States.*

The spruce grouse is slightly larger than other grouse. It perches in conifers and often allows hunters to get very close.

A male spruce grouse, with its two characteristic red wattles.

BEHAVIOR

The spruce grouse often flies out from under the hunter's feet and perches at the top of a small tree a few meters away. Basically, hunting this bird does not incite much interest.

HUNTING THE SPRUCE GROUSE

With its behavior halfway between that of a partridge and that of a grouse, the spruce grouse spends most of its time pacing around its territory. Hunting it with a pointer is the most interesting method.

All pointer breeds are suitable, although dogs with a flair for tracking are especially useful. A capricious bird, the spruce grouse will on one day allow itself to be blockaded easily, while the very next day it will run and become impossible to approach, even with skilled dogs.

Hazel Grouse

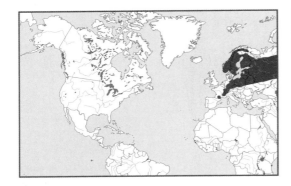

LATIN NAME:
Bonasa bonasia

With its exemplary discretion and the disconcerting ease with which it can slalom between tree trunks or run away through the shrubs, the hazel grouse is small for a grouse but still manages to arouse all of the hunter's senses.

DESCRIPTION

About the size of a partridge, the hazel grouse is distinguished both by a russet and gray belly marked with black and white, and by a black throat bordered with white. The plumage of the male is more colorful than that of the female.

HABITAT

Living in the forested massifs of much of Europe (the southeast of France marks the western limits of its distribution zone), the hazel grouse is found from France to Siberia via Scandinavia. It

The hazel grouse is a forest bird that flees from danger by running away.

is a species that lives chiefly in woodland at altitudes ranging from 330 ft. (100 m) to more than 6560 ft. (2000 m). It prefers a mixed forest of broadleaf trees and conifers, with undergrowth stocked with shrubby vegetation.

DIET

The hazel grouse's diet consists of leaves, buds, berries, and seeds, but it also eats insects and worms during warm weather. Apart from what is preserved of its basic diet by the cold in winter, the hazel grouse eats tree branches and bark.

HUNTING THE HAZEL GROUSE

A meeting rather than a search

The hazel grouse is a disconcerting bird: most of the time it is shy and retiring but sometimes it reveals a surprisingly provocative, even naive, attitude. Because of this, many hunters think of it as an "encounter bird" and not as a bird to be specifically sought out. A quick shooter will have enough time when he meets hazel grouse to knock over one or two of them. Sometimes, even the slow-

---

AN AMERICAN HAZEL GROUSE

The ruffed grouse (*Bonasa umbellus*) can be found throughout Canada, in the north of the United States, and in part of Alaska. It is clearly larger than the hazel grouse. Nevertheless, both birds have identical preferences, with forests, preferably mixed ones, forming the principal habitat. The population densities of these birds can be extraordinary.

---

est of hunters has enough time to take aim at a bird that has come and sat right in front of him.

In some areas where it is abundant, such as Russia, Canada, and southern Alaska, the hazel grouse is hunted by ambush both morning and evening, especially near water sources.

Hunting with pointers

Precisely because it has this unpredictable side to its behavior, the most sporting way to hunt hazel grouse is with a pointer.

In fact, these dogs have to work hard to corner this bird, which either runs off or takes to the trees. Very often, dogs that are good with hunting woodcock will succeed here. Solid points from the dogs are rare, so the hunter needs

strong vigilance and fast reflexes to get the shot off quickly.

HUNTING PLACES

In western Europe, the French, Italian, and German hunting areas offer some opportunities, but the more interesting sectors have an unequal distribution of birds, and numbers are sometimes weak. In the east, especially in the Russian taiga where millions of birds are culled, most forest coverts offer exceptional possibilities. Finally, southern Alaska and Canada (most notably Quebec and Gaspé) are known for their fabulous population densities.

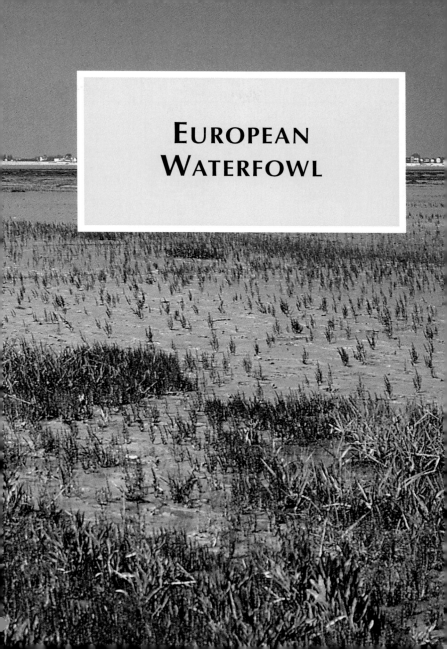

EUROPEAN
WATERFOWL

Ducks and Geese

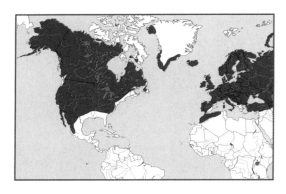

GEESE
GENUS NAME: *Anser*

**BARNACLE/
CANADA GEESE**
GENUS NAME: *Branta*

DUCKS, TEAL
GENUS NAME: *Anas*

MERGANSERS
GENUS NAME: *Mergus*

Several dozen species of ducks and geese can be found across Europe and North America, some of them appearing on both continents depending on the time of year. This extraordinary diversity makes hunting them so interesting.

DESCRIPTION

Rather than describing in detail more than 40 species of ducks and geese, we will concentrate on the common features of these birds.

For ducks and geese, water is an indispensable element, whether as a place to rest or as a feeding area.

Pochard.

The first things that the observer notices about one of these birds in flight are the long neck, short tail, and great ease of movement coupled with considerable power. Other obvious characteristics are a rounded shape, a lively eye, and a flat, large bill. Among surface-feeding ducks, a marked sexual dimorphism is evident, with the males often clad in sumptuous and richly colored feathers that are a far cry from the often unobtrusive and camouflaged plumage of the females.

Both sexes have colored wing flashes (the speculum) with precise outlines, one of the identifying marks for this subfamily of birds.

THE MAIN FAMILIES OF DUCKS AND LARGE GEESE

Ducks and geese can be broadly classified according to their general behavior and how they feed.

Surface-feeding ducks

These ducks remain on the surface of the water to feed, dipping little more than their heads under water. When taking flight, they leave the surface immediately. The diet for these birds is essentially vegetarian.

Examples: mallard, shoveler, pintail, gadwall, Barbary or Muscovy duck, marbled teal, blue-winged teal, garganey, and common or green-winged teal.

Diving ducks

Unlike surface-feeding ducks, these ducks dive completely under water to feed. They also run along the surface of the water for quite a long time, to gain speed when attempting to take flight.

Pintail.

Greylag geese.

Examples: pochard, tufted duck, scaup, ring-necked duck, red-crested pochard, common goldeneye, white-winged scoter, and common scoter.

Geese

Large geese, which often live in large, noisy colonies, have elongated necks. They feed almost exclusively on land, often using the water as an area for rest and refuge.

Examples: greylag goose, white-fronted goose, pink-footed goose, snow goose, bean goose, and lesser white-fronted goose.

Barnacle/Canada geese

These birds resemble other geese in every way except in that they are generally smaller. They are also quite gregarious and feed in a way similar to other geese.

Examples: Canada goose, brant goose, barnacle goose, and red-breasted goose.

Mergansers

Mergansers are the only "ducks" (along with divers and grebes) that do not have a flat bill. Instead, they have thin, long bills. These birds are divers that feed chiefly on fish.

Examples: goosander, red-breasted merganser, and smew.

Goosander.

Long spells of freezing weather often force ducks to migrate to milder places.

HABITAT

Whether in a simple pond or the ocean, ducks need water. In water, they find the essentials of their diet. Ducks love both aquatic plants and plankton, and use their bills to nibble food and to filter water. This is why surface-feeding ducks, particularly the teal, choose shallow feeding areas, while bay ducks are suited to water of various depths. When not feeding, ducks of all kinds may float above deep waters (such as a sea, large lake, or river). Floating far from the water's edge provides the security of not being surprised during an inactive phase. Geese have a more terrestrial nature but are not averse to water. The goose's diet consists of grasses and seeds that it locates while foraging on land. Water provides a quiet area in which to wash and groom its plumage.

Mallard are constantly on the move, and thus there are large populations in many European countries.

DUCKS AND GEESE OF EUROPE AND NORTH AMERICA

This list names the most common ducks and geese only.

The barnacle goose, clearly smaller in size than its cousin the Canada goose, is often found in Scandinavia.

Mallard (*Anas platyrhynchos*)
Northern shoveler (*Anas clypeata*)
Pintail (*Anas acuta*)
Gadwall (*Anas strepera*)
European wigeon (*Anas penelope*)
American wigeon (*Mareca americana*)
Barbary or Muscovy duck (*Cairina moschata*)
Garganey (*Anas querquedula*)
Common or green-winged teal (*Anas crecca*)
Blue-winged teal (*Anas discors*)
Cinnamon teal (*Anas cyanoptera*)
Marbled teal (*Marmaronetta angustirostris*)
Common or European shelduck
(*Tadorna tadorna*)
Ruddy shelduck (*Tadorna ferruginea*)
Tufted duck (*Aythya fuligula*)
Common pochard
(*Aythya ferina*)
Greater scaup
(*Aythya marila*)
Ferruginous duck
(*Aythya nycora*)
Ring-necked duck
(*Aythya collaris*)
Redhead (*Aythya americana*)

Lesser scaup (*Aythya affinis*)
Red-crested pochard (*Netta rufina*)
Common goldeneye (*Bucephala clangula*)
Harlequin duck (*Histrionicus histrionicus*)
White-winged scoter (*Melanitta fusca*)
Common scoter (*Melanitta nigra*)
American eider (*Somateria mollissima*)

Greylag goose (*Anser anser*)
White-fronted goose (*Anser albifrons*)
Snow goose (*Chen caerulesceus*)
Bean goose (*Anser fabalis*)
Lesser white-fronted goose
(*Anser erythropus*)
Pink-footed goose
(*Anser fabalis brachyrhynchus*)
Canada goose (*Branta canadensis*)
Barnacle goose (*Branta leucopsis*)
Brant goose (*Branta bernicla*)

Mallard.

Canada goose.

Mudflats and other places with shallow water attract surface-feeding ducks.

Areas of rest and feeding zones

Many ducks and geese are actively nocturnal feeders, although this does not prevent them from feeding during the day. These birds require successive rest areas and feeding zones. Feeding zones often cover a vast area (such as a large stretch of water, sea, or inaccessible section of river) that is free of danger and allows them to rest. Some of these birds leave their coverts in the evening to return, under cover of darkness, to the feeding areas that are more exposed. The birds feed for a good portion of the night, frequently and noisily changing sector. Just before dawn, the majority of the birds return to the refuge, while a few birds remain in the area. These birds prefer an impenetrable, reedy marsh, mangrove swamp, or pool, where they can move about undisturbed, even in broad daylight. Geese will behave in exactly the same manner, although they sometimes wait until night falls before going off to feed. The flooded meadows, farmland, or moors that they frequent are often very exposed, which explains their cautiousness.

BEHAVIOR

Great wariness and highly developed senses

Any hunter who wants to approach ducks or geese in their natural habitats – even without planning to actually hunt them – will notice their extraordinary wariness. The hearing and vision of these birds (sometimes even the sense of smell) are wonderfully efficient. Some ducks (especially the mallard) give the appearance of true intelligence as they quickly make the distinction between a danger zone (hunting area) and a refuge zone (reserve).

Aquatic plants always signal that surface feeders are around.

Ducks and Geese

Canada goose.

REPRODUCTION

Most ducks and geese nest either on the ground or just above the water, and their eggs are exposed to all sorts of risks (such as predators and changes in water level). Almost all of the young leave the nest quickly and find safety on the water, escorted by the mothers. Different nesting habits have been noted, such as those of ducks that nest in the hollows of trees, in the crevices of cliffs, or (in the case of shelduck) in abandoned burrows. If the brood or the eggs are destroyed, the mother almost automatically replaces them with another clutch.

HUNTING DUCKS AND GEESE

Pass shooting

Shooting ducks and geese in flight, the most suitable method of hunting them, involves the hunter's positioning himself in the flight path at the beginning and end of the day. Generally speaking, hunters take up their shooting positions along the axis between the daytime resting areas and the nocturnal feeding zones (and vice versa).

These birds will neither go to any particular feeding zone nor travel via any particular route. Anyone is, of course, free to position himself behind the first clump of reeds he comes to in the hopes of seeing some ducks come by within range.

WATCH OUT FOR LOCAL LAWS

In different countries, any particular duck or goose may either be on the list of species that can be hunted or be subject to partial or total protection. This is particularly true of brent geese, which are protected in France but may be hunted in North America, eastern Europe, or Scandinavia. In addition, many birds may be shot only during a precisely defined season. The hunter should always seek information about the local laws. Some change almost every year, especially in western Europe.

The end of the day is the best time to see ducks in action.

The wise hunter is sure to take up his position well before dusk.

Seeing formations of geese is always a memorable event during the hunting season.

The evening flight

In regards to the evening flight, it is preferable to use a rough shoot or make a simple visit to inspect the edges of pools and marshes, to understand the recent movements of the birds. The hunter can clearly see the places near shallow water where mud and grasses have been disturbed.

He can also find loose feathers, because ducks and geese regularly groom their plumage. The hunter should establish himself near these places, or between them and the resting area, for the evening flight. For geese, he should position himself between the resting area and a cornfield or water meadow that the birds visit.

Ducks and Geese

The morning flight is rarely in the same place as the evening one.

The morning flight

The hunter may be tempted to assume he can use the same methods in the morning, but it actually depends upon a few factors. If the evening hunt is fruitful, there is a good chance that the same spot will be deserted for the rest of the night. There will be no birds left in the morning, and the hunter risks disappointment. It is useful for the hunter to know several feeding zones, so that he can position himself between those that have not been disturbed and the resting place. The hunter can organize his morning hunt better if he happened to be near the birds during the previous evening. He will then have a better idea of where to intercept them returning at dawn the next day.

Shooting

During evening and morning flights, the birds sometimes fly low and suddenly land close by. The hunter might not see anything, but he can distinctly hear the birds arriving on the water. He must then keep down for as long as possible, making use of the weak light mirrored on the water to make out the wake lines, and then fire at the

THE IMPORTANCE OF THE WIND

Ducks spend a good portion of the day on water and are very sensitive to the wind: waves disturb them, and the noise that they produce within the vegetation on the banks keeps them in a state of insecurity. Violent wind causes ducks to become frantic, flying in all directions, resting momentarily on small ponds and the sheltered parts of rivers, and then suddenly taking off together again, only to return later. These can be memorable hunting days for the hunter wearing waders, who will be surprised to find himself flushing ducks in places that are usually deserted. These conditions offer the rare opportunity to see ducks in flight for much of the day, or at least for a much longer segment of the day than usual.

On windy days, sheltered pools surrounded by woods are good places to find ducks.

Ducks and Geese

point of the "V" shape on the water. In early morning, birds in flight are considered in range when their dark shapes become distinguishable, often less than 27 or 33 yd. (25 or 30 m) away. The hunter should not use a shotgun that is too heavily choked, because it is difficult to take aim in such dim light. As the sky brightens, however, he often has a chance to shoot at birds flying about 40 yards away. In this situation, he should use a shotgun that produces a tighter shot pattern.

Weapons and ammunition

Either a double-barreled gun (1/2 and full choke) or a semi-automatic gun (3/4 choke) will make an acceptable compromise. The ammunition depends upon the time of year and the species. Ducks with summer plumage at the beginning of the season are hunted with No. 6 and No. 7 shot. Later in the season, the hunter should use No. 5 and No. 6 shot. When teal are flying low with the wind, it is better to use cartridges of No. 7 and No. 8 shot with a vegetable-fiber wad (instead of the usual all-plastic type) to get broader patterns at close range. With geese, the choice is always between No. 2 and No. 4 shot.

Waterfowl hunting requires the proper equipment.

The dog

Shooting birds in flight without a good dog trained in retrieving is very risky. The Labrador retriever, the golden retriever, and the flat-coated retriever (or any other breed accustomed to retrieving in water) are helpful in both bringing back the dead birds and pursuing the wounded ones.

The blind

This term describes "lying-in-wait" hunting methods, except for the predictable morning and evening flights. The hunter's position is often quite elaborate and comfortable, because the duration of the ambush is not limited to periods at the end of the day. The blind is set up beside a stretch of water or tidal reservoir and is well concealed, blending in perfectly with the countryside. It is equipped with apertures used to watch the movements of the birds.

This kind of hunting sometimes includes positioning decoys and live callers (birds) a fair distance from the hide. Waiting within a blind may take a long time, so it is better to work with two or three hunters who take turns keeping watch and remaining vigilant.

Hidden within the reeds, the hunter increases his chances by using a call.

wood, decoys today are almost always constructed out of plastic. Each one has a small ring, to which a length of cord is fixed. At the end of the cord is a weight that acts as an anchor yet leaves the decoy free to bob about in the wind and waves. Some decoys are painted with the colors and markings of the species they imitate, while others are more fantastic or are left completely undecorated.

There are no great differences from one decoy to another, but mimicry of nature is very important. For example, decoys with holes, those that are lopsided, or those covered in frost act like scarecrows, frightening the birds away.

Decoys

Ducks have superior vision and can see other ducks resting on water from long distances away. Because of a gregarious nature, they will usually land nearby, reassured by the sight of other ducks. This is where the idea of using decoys came from. The decoys are models that more or less faithfully imitate some representative species from the place being hunted, according to the season. Originally made from

Blinds are often comfortable and fitted with apertures for watching the resting places of birds.

Ducks and Geese

Shooting from an ambush – where this practice is allowed – is most productive at dawn and at dusk.

Some of these decoys do not look natural and may prevent birds from landing.

12 gauge with 1/2 and full choke) and another for long-range shooting (such as a 10 gauge with full choke). Most ducks are hunted with No. 5 and No. 6 shot, but geese require something between No. 2 and No. 4 shot.

Live callers

Some hunters also resort to using live ducks to reinforce the attractive powers of the decoy. Both evocative postures and musical qualities make these decoys so useful. Of course, not all live ducks are effective, and they must be rigorously selected. When it comes to calling, female ducks are most frequently used. A female that "sings" well can divert passing ducks, even those far away, and she will probably induce them to land. This practice is allowed in some countries but not in others. Similarly, it is illegal to keep certain species in captivity. Another use for live ducks is to release one or two toward a distant formation. If these "traitors" have been

trained well, they will join the formation and then guide it to the resting place located near the blind.

Firing

Firing is sometimes done at long ranges. Since this hunt is conducted from a fixed position, it is best to have one shotgun for short to medium ranges, (such as a

Stalking

Stalking refers to the different strategies that hunters use when moving toward the birds until an effective firing range is reached. Stalking on land is often tedious and usually

The wire-haired terrier is efficient in the woods, on the plain and also on moorland.

Ducks and Geese

Stalking by boat may surprise a few ducks along the banks, but the shooter must be quick.

ends in repeated failure. Stalking on water, although also problematic, does produce better results.

The boat

The hunter can disguise a small boat with fallen branches and rushes, and drift down to the resting place on the river. In the marshes or backwaters, one hunter can push the boat while the other hunter, in the forward position, prepares to shoot.

In northern Europe and the southeast of France, birds resting at sea are stalked with the help of a craft inspired by the kayak, which is masked by the waves. The hunter must be in excellent physical condition to lie stretched out in such an uncomfortable and unstable position.

The horse

In France, waterfowl do not seem to be afraid of animals that are not predators, and so stalking geese can also be done with the help of a horse! The hunter walks behind the horse in order to disguise his movements, stopping within firing range. The horse must be well trained enough to ignore the sound of the gun going off. In some instances, hunters operate in pairs with the help of a life-sized, wooden model of a horse. Although fascinating, these stalking methods are more the exception than the rule in being truly representative of hunting techniques.

Rough shooting

Ducks and geese are not the types of birds to be speci-

Going down rivers and streams in a boat can get the hunter closer to waterfowl, but these hunters are not being very unobtrusive.

Ducks and Geese

fically sought out in a rough shoot, also called "jump shooting." The hunter beats marshes and reedy areas to flush out young, first-year duck, which can now fly but are more inclined to remain in cover and stay out of reach of their pursuers. Rough shooting is practiced in countries where legislation allows for the season to begin during the summer when young birds are plentiful. However, the hunter must ask himself whether it is a good idea to hunt young birds whose defensive abilities are nothing like those of adult birds. After the summer season, however, rough shooting can bring both surprises and great feelings. Ducks may be surprised while exploring the banks of a small stream, approaching small ponds surrounded by tall reeds or, very simply, coming within good range because they have just been startled out of their cover.

At the beginning of the season, a pointing dog will bring excellent results with young mallard.

Rough shooting can be exhausting and requires a good knowledge of the territory.

The right place at the right time

A hunter who knows his land well and uses this as an advantage can improve this unpredictable method of hunting. For example, he can choose rainy or windy days when the birds use only basic cover (water-holes, rivers, ditches, and sheltered peat bogs). He must dress in neutral colors and make as little noise as possible when pushing past vegetation. Then, while approaching likely areas and using a good breeze, the hunter must maintain his concentration and not be surprised by a sudden, noisy takeoff. Finally, it is essential that any retriever used is well trained, obedient, and attentive.

HUNTING PLACES
Romania

Eastern Romania, located near the Black Sea and the Danube River delta, is a favored site for ducks passing over and stopping to rest. It is an obligatory migration route from the beginning of October. The plains between Bucharest and the Bulgarian frontier host large numbers of geese during that period.

Russia

In Russia, the Volga River creates a gigantic delta, a true labyrinth of several thousand acres of water and

Rough shooting along riverbanks can produce surprises.

Ducks and Geese

On a rough shoot, the hunter must be ready to get the shot off quickly.

floodplains. Beginning in September, birds from a large part of Russia (especially from Siberia) stop to rest in the Volga delta. A dozen different species can be identified within a single flight.

Ireland
Beside immense lakes (such as the loughs of Derg, Ree, Mask, Corrib, and Erne) and the River Shannon, Ireland has tens of thousands of wild lakes, water meadows, and innumerable peat bogs that shelter (notably from September to November) thousands of ducks, especially incredible squadrons of common teal.

Canada
Canada is an immense country filled with waterways, harboring a mass of waterfowl species that, from the end of August, assemble in large numbers.

During cold spells, ducks can be found only on running water.

A boat is indispensable for the hunter who does not use a good retriever.

In Quebec alone, there are several million lakes, areas of tundra, and water meadows that are favored by passing geese. Sea ducks, such as the American eider, gather along hundreds of miles of the St. Lawrence River.

France

With its varied countryside and diversity of habitats, France has no lack of paradises for waterfowl, such as the Poitou marshes, the pools of the Dombes region, the Bassin d'Arcachon, or Camargue Island.

In most countries, pass shooting is the most effective way to hunt duck.

Common Snipe

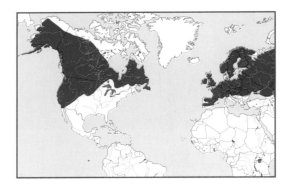

LATIN NAME:
Capella gallinago

With a head that is clearly like that of the woodcock, the snipe is the waterfowl that hunters talk about most. The most representative of the species is the marsh-dwelling common snipe, which lovers of pointing dogs hunt with great enthusiasm.

DESCRIPTION

Resembling a miniature woodcock, the snipe is a slender bird with an extremely long bill about 3 in. (7 cm) in length. Its back is a mixture of brown, russet, and beige barred with white. The belly is pale, and the tail forms a

A star among the mud-dwellers, the snipe is enthusiastically hunted in many countries.

Snipe always like the edges of pools where grass is not too tall.

small wheel outlined with russet. The snipe's takeoff is astonishingly rapid, and is accompanied by sudden swerves that add a characteristic rasping sound. In flight, the angled wings are long and pointed and give the bird great speed and elegance. In spite of its small size, the snipe is a long-distance traveler, with migrations that take it from Russia to Spain and from Scandinavia to Africa. Like almost all of the mud-dwellers, snipe nest on the ground. Without their greatly camouflaged plumage, many chicks would be lost, since they cannot fly properly until they are five to six weeks old.

HABITAT

The life of the snipe is bound to water: riverbanks, the edges of pools, water meadows, mudflats, marsh-

The water level is what decides if the snipe will settle. Snipe must be able to move around and bury their bills effectively in the mud.

land, drainage ditches, and tiny streams. The water should not be deeper than 1 or 2 in. (3 or 4 cm), allowing the birds to move about and root in the soil with their bills. Even though marshland hosts a large number of these birds, the snipe's distribution is quite fragmented. During migration, any suitable terrain, including small peat bogs, flooded meadows, and the edges of small mountain streams, will attract a few birds.

Generally speaking, the snipe is quite picky about the quality of the terrain, and it prefers areas with cattle or horses. These birds like to be near droppings,

Common Snipe

which are a constant source of easily harvested insects and larvae.

BEHAVIOR

Snipe feed by digging their bills into the earth or mud, and thus long freezing spells

channels, ditches, or the edges of rivers and streams when the freeze is severe.

Cattle keep wetlands in perfect condition, and snipe are never far away!

HUNTING SNIPE
Rough shooting

Walking around the marshes or trying a flooded meadow or small peat bog, the rough shooter will flush out a few snipe. Of course, a hunter who knows his

can be catastrophic for them. The only option then is to flee to more hospitable areas, provided the journey is not too long or difficult from a climatic point of view. They might also survive if they can make do with some other form of running water, such as

Sharp spells of cold always bring heavy losses among snipe, and some of them die because they are not able to eat properly. In addition, their defensive capabilities are clearly reduced, causing the birds to fall prey to numerous predators.

terrain intimately will take care to tackle the likely areas, upwind and fully alert. Lacking the valuable faculties of a dog, the hunter is almost always surprised by the abruptness with which these birds take off. Shooting is instinctive, and the swing must be very

All wetlands, however small, attract a few birds.

wide to allow for the target's speed. It is also possible to go rough shooting within a group of five or six, with each hunter keeping well apart from the others and thus creating more shooting opportunities. Because the shooting is often low to the ground, each participant must remain calm. Efficient retrieving dogs are indispensable, because it is difficult to find a snipe in the reeds or grass without their assistance.

Hunting with pointers
Hunters who love a big quest and fine actions and have a taste for statuesque

---

OTHER SNIPE

In addition to the common snipe, the species most frequently encountered around the world, hunters can find other snipe in the wetlands. Their requirements in terms of habitat and diet are identical.

European jack snipe
(Lymnocryptes minimus)
Almost half the size of its cousin from the marshes, it has the same color of plumage but has a bill that is 1 in. (3 cm) shorter. It takes off less rapidly and at more nearly a right angle. The jack snipe is known in France as the "deaf snipe," due to the way it often takes off just as

the hunter is about to step on it! Jack snipe and common snipe are often found living close to each other.

Great snipe
(Gallinago media)
The great snipe is very similar to the common snipe, although it is slightly larger in size. When at rest, it is difficult to identify using just its shape. When this bird is in flight, it is obvious that the underside of the tail is much lighter. Of the three snipe, the great snipe is the least represented.

Jack snipe.

Common Snipe

WHICH DOG FOR SNIPE?

The owners of British breeds and the lovers of Continental dogs have been in dispute about this for many years. A passionate hunting dog that is often put in against snipe will hunt the bird correctly, whatever breed the dog may be. Despite this, practice shows that British dogs (pointers and setters) have more talent for this kind of hunting than do other breeds. This is due to the power of their noses and the often decisive way that they run and fix the bird at an ideal range. For some years, Brittany spaniels, strongly infused with British blood, have developed a similar search technique, and many of these dogs perform very well on snipe. Moreover, they often have an advanced taste for retrieving, which makes them extremely useful in the marshes. The dogs that have a precise idea of the position of the bird and of how to keep a safe distance enable their companions to shoot a lot of snipe.

dogs will enjoy hunting snipe. The snipe has a light scent and a rapid takeoff; getting close to it is often a delicate business. Because of these factors, the dogs must exhibit the requisite qualities. Apart from good noses, they must possess an intensive and methodical searching method that enables them to explore the ground thoroughly. More-over, they must be enter-prising, because snipe will not tolerate any indecisive-ness on the part of a dog. Generally, the dogs special-izing in this bird freeze for only a short time, and then they aggressively run to fix the bird from a useful distance. Only with fre-quent practice will these dogs ever be able to excel with snipe. Consequently, there are days when no dog is able to point a single bird.

Shooting

The snipe is not the easiest bird to shoot, but achieving an honorable percentage of success is not unattainable. When the dog fixes the bird, the hunter must act appro-priately. The instinctive hunter will shoot as soon as the bird rises, while the more methodical hunter will allow the bird to get some distance away and cover it broadly before shooting. From a purely ballistic point of view, the second method should have a better chance, because between 33 and 44 yd. (30 and 40 m), the shot has a wider pattern. The first shooter needs a weapon whose first barrel produces a wide pattern, while the second should choose barrels that produce a relatively concentrated pattern at a longer range.

The battue

It is possible to hunt snipe by battue in small groups or larger parties. The shooters line up in prearranged positions, or conceal themselves behind a tamarisk hedge or in the reeds. A walking team, accompanied by dogs, beats the marshes, the peat bogs, or the flooded pastures to flush as many birds as they can. The wind plays an important role in this type of hunting, with the birds almost automatically taking off. The intelligence of the group and the placing of the guns are thus essential.

Shooting

Although this method of hunting is not considered very sporting, shooting snipe that are moving at top speed is not always easy. The only advantage to be gained from this type of

It is easy to understand why the snipe has a long bill once it is seen feeding.

Common Snipe

shooting is that the sudden jerks of the snipe are clearly less disconcerting: while the bird is changing direction, the shooter has time to aim his shot properly.

Ammunition

The ideal ammunition is a combination of No. 7 and No. 8 shot, keeping in mind the long ranges being used and the effects of the wind.

With an innate retrieving sense and a soft mouth, the Labrador is an excellent retriever of snipe from all locations.

The dogs

Shooters try to use good retrievers, such as the Labrador, golden, and flat-coated, which will retrieve game as they go along. If the dogs are not to intervene until the end of the hunt, the shooters must memorize the number of birds they hit and as many of the landing places as possible, in order to guide the retrievers later.

For shooting snipe, the shotgun and ammunition must be suited to the task.

WHICH SHOT FOR SNIPE?

Small shot (No. 8 or No. 9) is recommended, to allow for the vulnerability of the bird's large wing area. On windy days, it is better to choose a slightly larger shot (No. 7 to No. 7.5) to secure a more reliable trajectory for the pattern in the air. Despite its reputation for being a fragile bird, the snipe can carry one or two small shot without automatically falling. Unfortunately, the hunter can calculate where the bird was hit only by observing its flight path.

The snipe is fairly fragile, but the ambient conditions require the hunter to select his ammunition well.

HUNTING PLACES
Ireland

Enjoying a climate tempered by damp maritime winds, Ireland harbors so many peat bogs, marshes, and meadows by pools and rivers that it is difficult, especially during October and November, not to flush snipe in quantity.

The charm of hunting in Ireland hinges on the fact that while hunting other game (pheasant, hare, and woodcock), hunters regularly cross areas containing a few snipe.

Spain

To the south of Barcelona, the Ebro River delta is a stopping point much prized by waterfowl, and it forms an important zone for birds in transit and for others that are resting. Snipe congregate there in large numbers. This habitat is made up of marshes, open shores, and wetlands. They can be hunted in waders or with a pointer.

Quebec

In Quebec, all of the water meadows beside rivers or tundra scattered with small lakes and marshy areas are

This hunter happily displays the snipe he skillfully shot in the southeast of Ireland.

Rhône River delta, and the marshes of Picardy to the peat bogs of the Massif Central, France is favored by snipe and migratory birds.

The first movements start in September, but it is in

host to large contingents of snipe, which are often little hunted. In many areas, it is better to use the services of a guide. Hunting with pointers is widespread, notably in October when the dogs hunt both snipe in the wetlands and woodcock in the surrounding forests.

France

From the shores of the north to the wetlands of the

Snipe often exert the same fascination on the wildfowler as woodcock do on the woodland hunter.

Even the smallest marshes are visited by a few snipe.

October, November, and sometimes December that the greatest numbers arrive. In France, these birds are hunted as much by general hunters as by those specializing in hunting with pointers.

Waders

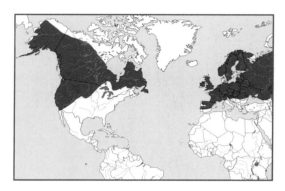

Sometimes ignored and always rated far behind the snipe, waders nevertheless offer an interesting diversity and unforeseeable encounters. This is most agreeable when, for instance, duck hunting has not been very rewarding.

Large pools, enclosed by broad, open banks and mudflats, attract many shore birds (shown here are plovers).

DESCRIPTION
Belonging to the immense family of wading birds, waders often have a slender silhouette, with thin, long legs and bill. This shape is directly related to their dietary habits, enabling them to move about effortlessly in the mud and shallow waters. Most waders nest on the ground in nests that are often more than perfunctory, and the fledglings, with their perfectly camouflaged plumage, remain in the nest. There is no shortage of waders subspecies, and they come in such a variety of shapes that it is always a surprise when the hunter comes across one.

HABITAT
The thing that most characterizes the family of waders (to which snipe also belong) is the strong tendency to live in wetlands, such as marshes, estuaries, riverbanks, mudflats, and the seashore. All of these areas are good for them, as long as the water level is not

Most waders nest on the ground, where the eggs are exposed to predators.

too deep and they can dig up their food (worms, larvae, mollusks, and insects). Another common characteristic is extraordinarily gregarious behavior, which accounts for the sometimes impressive gatherings of hundreds or thousands of birds just before the migratory departures.

Among the waders, there exist some birds that occupy a place apart. Such is the curlew, a large bird with a long bill that is curved near the tip and with a unique, gloomy call. Curlew are always difficult to approach and rarely allow themselves to be surprised. The lapwing is another waders that is almost impossible to get near.

HUNTING WADERS
All waterfowl hunters will sooner or later find themselves in the presence of various waders, and hunting them can be approached in different ways.

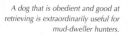

A dog that is obedient and good at retrieving is extraordinarily useful for mud-dweller hunters.

Waders

Hunting with waders, in a battue, and with pass shooting

The wildfowl hunter who operates while wearing waders at the edge of a large pool, in a maritime area, or on a flooded pasture will be pleasantly surprised to meet lapwing, plover, godwit, and other birds. Generally speaking, these birds have very good vision and often take off out of range. Favorable opportunities present themselves when several hunters beat the

Lapwing sometimes gather in large numbers and are actively sought by hunters.

same sector and send each other birds. Pass shooting is also possible during the migratory period, with the hunter taking care to position himself in line with the most probable arrival

The curlew (here with a female mallard and a snipe) is a choice catch for many wildfowlers.

zones (those that lead to beaches and mudflats and offer the best conditions).

The ambush

For regular success, there is nothing like hunting by ambush, which can be done from a blind or other structure completely covered with sand, earth, or mud. Stationed near ponds, shores, or mudflats, this type of position is more effective if decoys are randomly put down, capturing the attention of the waders from afar. Shooting is then conducted from an effective range because the birds have already stopped nearby.

LEARN TO IDENTIFY THEM

Mudflats and shallow shores are much-favored resting places for sandpiper, plover, and other waders.

Among the waders, some birds are protected. The first concern is to learn to recognize them to avoid making errors of identification. This is not a problem with the black-and-white oystercatcher, the curlew with its long, curved bill, and the crested lapwing. With other birds, however, there may be confusion. There is nothing like practice and observation, and a birdwatcher's manual is a good idea. After that, habit and knowledge should suffice. If you are ever in doubt, don't shoot.

France, some examples are the shores of the North Sea, the Somme River, the Gironde estuary, and Camargue Island. In Spain, there is the Ebro River delta. The shores of Ireland, where birds frequently gather in the thousands, is also an excellent spot. On the north coast of Quebec, within the tundra zones riddled with ponds and along the open banks of the St. Lawrence River, the chances of an encounter are also very high, and the diversity of species is often unbelievable.

When the meadows are partly flooded, lapwing often arrive in large numbers and spend the days looking for earthworms. It is useless to try and approach them in the open. Instead, find out where the resting place is (often on a small rise), erect an unobtrusive blind, and put out some decoys. This is the only way to get a shot at any of these wary birds.

HUNTING PLACES

All wetlands and shores, which encourage birds to settle, are host to large numbers of waders. In

Waders are very alert, and it is essential for the hunter to conceal himself well.

Index

Page numbers in Roman type refer to text entries; numbers in *italic* type to illustrations, captions, and panels; and numbers in **bold** type to the place where the topic is mainly treated.

Photography credits

Anagnostidis/NATURE: 220-221 – **Berthon/NATURE:** 69 t, 119, 171 t – **Berthoule/NATURE:** 46, 92 l, 174, 238, 240 t – **Buttin/NATURE:** 22 b, 23 b, 24, 25 b, 26, 27, 43, 52 r, 53 tl, 55, 61 r, 71 t, 72 m, 75, 82-83, 86 t, 90 b, 93 t, 105 t, 109 b, 110 t, 110 b, 111, 113 t, 114, 115 t, 117 t, 117 b, 129 t, 176 r, 176 l, 181 t, 184 t, 185 t, 185 b, 187 t, 187 b, 195 b, 200 b, 222, 223 t, 227 t, 229, 247 b – **Chaumeton/NATURE:** 163 t, 215 t, 215 b – **Chèvre/NATURE:** 221 t – **Corel:** 132-133, 136, 140, 141 t, 141 b, 144, 149, 150, 151, 154 t, 159 r – **G. Cortay:** 165 t, 182, 183 t, 199, 203 t, 206, 207, 208, 217 b, 218 t, 241, 242-243, 242 t, 244 b, 246 t – **Durantel/NATURE:** 69 b, 84, 94, 95, 103 b, 106, 123, 124, 166 t, 166 b, 181 b, 188, 189, 200 t, 200 m, 202 t, 217 t, 219 b, 221 br, 223 b, 228, 230, 231 b, 232 t, 232 b, 233 b, 237 t, 240 b, 243 t – **Ferrero/NATURE:** 52 l, 53 b, 54, 63 b, 68, 72 b, 80 b, 125, 127 b – **Gohier/NATURE:** 154 b, 155 b, 191 b – **Guittard/NATURE:** 179, 231 t – **Henry/NATURE:** 205 b – **Huin/NATURE:** 253 t – **Krasnodebski/NATURE:** 85, 86 b, 87 t, 88 tl, 102, 118, 121 b, 169 t, 169 b, 175 r, 178 t, 184 b, 198 t, 210 – **La Tourette/NATURE:** 233 t – **Labat/NATURE:** 47 t, 66 t, 89, 120 – **Lamaison/NATURE:** 212-213 – **Lanceau/NATURE:** 72 t, 80 t, 121 t, 128 b, 131 t, 134-135, 138, 139 t, 146, 147, 153 t, 156, 216 b, 218 m – **Laval/NATURE:** 236 – **Le Gall/NATURE:** 38-39, 48 t, 48 b, 53 tr, 60 t, 60 b, 61 l, 62, 64, 65, 66 b, 70 t, 70 b, 71 b, 73 t, 73 b, 74 t, 74 b, 76, 78, 96, 97 t, 97 b, 100 t, 100 b, 101, 103 t, 104, 112 tl, 115 b, 160-161, 162, 164, 165 b, 167, 172 b, 173 b, 175 l, 177 t, 194, 195 t, 196 t, 196 b, 197 t, 197 b, 198 b, 201, 202-203, 225 t, 225 b, 226, 227 b, 245 b, 246 b, 247 t – **Losange:** 128 t – **Erich Marek:** 51 t, 63 t, 69 t, 77, 173 t, 178b – **Mayet/NATURE:** 105 b, 109 t, 112-113, 112 tr, 122, 159 b, 172, 186, 191 t, 204, 214, 218 b, 220 t, 235 b, 239, 244 t – **Meitz/NATURE:** 192, 205 t – **NATURE:** 14 t, 14 b, 15 t, 15 ml, 15 b, 16 t, 23 t, 25 t, 28, 29 b, 224 – **Pasquet/NATURE:** 10-11, 12, 13 r, 13 l, 15 mr, 17 r, 17 l, 18 t, 18 m, 18 b, 19 r, 19 m, 19 l, 20, 21, 22 t, 23 m, 29 tr, 29 tl, 30 b, 32, 34 t, 34 b, 35 t, 35 b, 37 t, 37 b – **Polking/NATURE:** 158 t – **Reille/NATURE:** 130, 157 m, 190, 191 m – **C. Rossignol:** 40, 41, 42, 44 t, 44 b, 45, 47 b, 49, 50 t, 50 b, 51 b, 56 t, 56 b, 57, 58, 59 b, 77, 79 t, 79 b, 81 – **Samba/NATURE:** 126, 127 t, 155 t, 216 t – **Sauer/NATURE:** 152, 163 b, 170, 177 m, 180, 183 b, 209, 219 b, 234, 237 b, 245 t – **Siegel/NATURE:** 87 b, 88 tr, 90 t, 91, 92 r, 93 b, 98-99, 107, 108, 131 b, 157 t, 168 – **Syvertsen/NATURE:** 158 m – **B. Thomson:** 137, 139 b, 143, 148, 153 b, 157 b, 193.